RESURRECTION

Joseph Brice

RESURRECTION

DEATH COULD NOT
HOLD HIM DOWN
HE IS THE RISEN KING

I AM THE RESURRECTION AND LIFE

JOSEPH BRICE

Dedication

This is a dedicated to all of those of the Kingdom of God, who love the Lord and are believers of Jesus Christ, who has been, lie on, betrayed, criticized, misunderstood, made a mockery of and talked about in the worse ways, but regardless of what, you are Still Standing! Continue in the faith and doing God's will. You have an awaited crown in glory… blessings and peace to you.

To my beautiful wife, I honor you first as a woman…a secure woman, who knows who she is and who's she is. You are loving, kind, considerate, strong, versatile, and impressively adaptive for God's purpose in your life. You are a true woman of God. I, in particular, love how you steal away to pray and spend time with God. Your love for the Lord is beautiful to see. You are such an encourager and supporter. For all you do, may God blow your mind with blessings. I love you relentlessly!

To all of my children, I pray you will all fulfill your purpose in life. To take your place in this world and help to make it better. God knew YOU, before you were in the womb and spoke to you…listen and remember. Let nothing and no one, deter you from the truth…its all you'll ever have that will never die. You were born for greatness, know who you are and what you've been taught concerning your God. How beautiful you are and love is meant for you to be…just love and it will love you back, someway…somehow…

Let this be your "Year of Fulfillment."
Tamara Lowe

Acknowledgment

Thanks, To my Kingdom Rights Family and Leaders: Janet Lopez-Brice, Howard Cottman, Shakia Quickley and Geneva Renee Cottman, you are the best and stronger than you might think. I love how you love the Lord. Keep the faith and soar.

To Tamara Lowe...you're the best, also Zack and Jullian for the impact you are having on my life and the Kingdom Builders Academy Family, you are the best demonstration of the love of God, while building his kingdom, right here on earth. I am learning so much and will never be the same again. You may never know how many people you have reached, and lives you have touched? It's powerful...eternal thanks! Blessings and Great is your reward!

To my Audition Coach Mary Lingeibach, you encouraged me to get it done, thanks. To my Inner Circle Coach, Kelly Hale and my Inner Circle Team, "Team Anointed " Lynnie, Toni, Pheonix, Bud, Cassandra, Estelle, and Marilyn, I am honored and blessed to be a part of this team. I'm seeing potential, turning into purpose right before my eyes and, how I am believing for great things to come. I pray for nothing, but the best for all of you and blessings...Thanks KBA!

To my wife, Janet's Kingdom sisters from The Potter's House School Of Ministry (PHSOM), Pastor Myrli Sanchez, Pastor Navita KJ Johnson-Belcher, Masesi Masilela (Canada), Kim Vargas (Canada), Prophetess Hurline McGee, Angela Nixon and Llisa Dorsey. Thank you for being the Women of God that you are. I am blessed and honored to be part of such a powerful, anointed and humble group of women. Iron sharpens Iron and I am glad that you guys challenge and pour into me the wisdom and love of God. Each one of you have withstood the test of time and I can't wait to see what and where God will take you next. May the Peace of God and the unity of his Holy Spirit be perpetual in your lives, Blessings to you and your families. Love you my sisters, from Janet and Joseph.

To Wayne and Paula Hoyle, and family, I am so honored to have met you Wayne, although it was under some very challenging circumstances. God works in mysterious ways for sure. I love how you're always thinking about your family and how to provide for better living. You are a good man and God Bless you my brother. Tell Frank I said, CONGRATULATIONS to him and his new Bride. He has always been a man of his word and has been blessed with a gift to effectively work with such diverse people. You are a man of integrity. Thanks for everything.

To Larond (Slim) Bozeman, I am so proud of you for fighting to live up to your vow that you made to God. Many people forget after they get what they want from Him. I know it gets hard so many times, but be relentless, steadfast and unmovable for what God has promised you. I pray Blessings to you and your Queen and those beautiful daughters of yours. Tell Tyree, I'm praying for him and God has not changed His mind...His love for him will never die.

To Douglas (Doug) and Kelli Potter, I love how you chose to love each other and your family. The enemy will not come after anything that doesn't have value. Your union carries great wealth! Keep God first and live your best life. I'm proud of you guys. Be relentless!

To all of the families who have lost love ones due to the Pandemic and those to War. We pray for all of you, who are alive to feel the pain of lost. There is no pain that God feel and can't heal. Trust and believe this, those who made it in heaven, to be with the Lord Jesus, would not want to come back here, for nothing in this world (no offense) although they really love. But there's no love ,who can compare.

They are having a BALL, right now! This may be a little hard to believe, but, once you have the privilege of going home, you quickly realize, "There's No Place Like Home!"

Listen Believers, This world is not our home. Be encouraged and keep God first, and when our time is up, then eternity begins...what joy you will have. So Live to Live again…

<u>Message From The Bishop</u>

There was a woman, who was accused of being caught in the *very* act of adultery, but they failed to bring the man.,(you cannot commit adultery by yourself.) Appearing to be righteous, the religious leaders brought her before Jesus to get his opinion of what her fate should be and they reiterated that she was caught in the very act of adultery. Not that they respected Jesus but they were trying to find a way to trip him up, because he had a great following of people. So they were attempting to sabotage him. Their thoughts was to tempt Jesus, because if he said, "Let her go" then he would be speaking against The Law of Moses, and if he said, "stone her" then the people would turn against him and stop following him.

When they approached Jesus he was on the ground writing in the dirt.

The religious leaders said, "According to the law, we are supposed to stone her to death, but what do you say Jesus?" Jesus looks up and says, "He, who is without sin, let him cast the first stone." One by one they began to drop the stones, from the eldest to the youngest."Where are your accusers, is there anyone here to condemn you?" Jesus asked. The woman looked up and said, "No" (because she was down bracing herself for the hitting of the stones). Well ,neither do I condemn you. Go, and sin no more?" "Listen to the wisdom of God……..It is timeless"

Social Media (Facebook, Twitter, Instagram, Youtube, etc.) has become our modern day stones. We shouldn't be so quick to join in and post negative things about people. We all have sinned, but not all of us have gotten caught. We as Christians and/or Believers, should be the positive in this World, not the negative. We are the lights of the World, not to blend in with darkness, or take part in it. Be merciful as if it were you being stoned! *BISHOP T.D. JAKES*

Reference

- UNIVERSITY OF BRISTOL
- NATIONAL GEOGRAPHIC

Preface

If Jesus is not the Son of God, The Messiah, The Resurrection, then who was he? Why would the "powers that be" of the entire world agree to start time over? Why?

What need was there to mess with time…to change time?

As people, we rarely can agree on anything, without controversy, because we are naturally opinionated. There's an innate nature of choice, so we exercise our rights to choose, whenever and whenever it's allowed. So, we vote, or if we disagree, we protest.

Time for the entire world and civilization, as they would know it, was about to change forever, and no protest? I'm talking about, every nation, every government, every race, every culture, around the entire world, was given a notice about "TIME", and it is about to start over and…nothing?

Jesus was tried, condemned, convicted and executed as a criminal. Let's take away religion for a minute. He was executed, like,"Hanging Until Dead, Gas Chamber, Electric Chair, Lethal Injection , these are just a few examples and methods of execution, you may be familiar with, those convicted of a crime, worthy of death and sentenced to die. Jesus was sentenced to die!

Well, Crucifixion was the Roman Government's method of execution.

When he came to this world he was on a schedule. He came to work and when he was finished, he died. He came on purpose, to fulfill his purpose. "No man takes my life, I lay it down, and if I lay it down, then, I will pick it back up again" Jesus said. John the Baptist, called him, " The Lamb of God, who comes to takes away the sins of the world."

During the period that Jesus was crucified it was Passover. Which means they were offering up blood sacrifices from sheep or lambs as the *Atonement* for their *sins* this is according to the Law of Moses. Question, Why would the Israelites (Jews) stop offering a blood sacrifice for their sins, according to the Law of Moses? What offering can they give God? Who could they offer up to God in their place, according to their law, or anyone for that fact? Answer, Jesus is the Lamb of God who came to take away the sins of the World. He was and Is the last and only sacrifice every needed for the atonement for humanity sins.   If Jesus is not the Messiah, Why would the entire World and the "Powers that be" agree to start time over for the entire World in honor of this man? Why wouldn't the Roman Empire (Government) or Caesar as an Emperor give themselves such a timeless and immortal honor, with time starting over?

Every time we schedule an appointment, go by calendar dates, celebrate holidays or birthdays and just day to day time of events we are acknowledging Jesus. Whether in knowledge or ignorance, believing or not, we are acknowledging Jesus as Lord, even if we are not serving him. Time started over in honor of this man, this God , who walked this earth. This is why I propose questions and answers in this book concerning B.C and A.D. and where it came from. We all know that the World is not 2000 plus years old. Every time we start a new calendar year, we are in celebration of his birthday date and his death date.

Jesus is presently sitting in Heavenly places, above all things in which he created. God put it in the hearts of men to do his will. Why didn't the Devil stop time from starting over? Answer, because we could not stop God. Blessed are all people who have excepted Jesus as Lord.

Kingdom is not a competition …it is supposed to be a completion. Yes, we do strive to for excellence and to be the best that we can be! But, at no time do we tear anyone down in the kingdom in order for us to come up. God will judge us. We are to love one another, if nobody else ever give us love. We are to be a people of love…not lust.

When God sends people into your life, he does not send them to compete with you, he sends them to help you to complete your purpose and assist yo in the fulfillment of your destiny. If they are competing with you, He did not send them and neither are they operating in the Spirit of God?

Some people unfortunately are married to their competition! Sometimes when people can't control you, they seek to sabotage or destroy you…and that's OK, as long you recognize it. We have many examples in the Bible of this, even what they did it to our Lord Jesus.

Judas, who was one of Jesus disciples (in-which the Lord had plans for him to sit on one of the 12 thrones in his kingdom), but Judas began competing with purpose. Both Judas and Jesus ended up hanging from a tree. Judas hanging saved nobody including himself, but on the other hand, Jesus hanging, saved the entire world of believers and Himself!

The enemy seduced Judas into believing he could use Jesus for a "come-up" but instead, he lost his place with God and his soul. If God called you, no one can take your place…even if they steal your position? Your place in God is secured!

Some people have been sent as assassins to your purpose. Know this; you are well equipped for the fight, just put on your whole amour of God (Ephesians 6: 10-19).

Be skillful with the WORD which is your sword and don't fight without your Shield (faith). Stand against that enemy and know who you are fighting! Recognize the Devil, even when he speaks through someone you may respect or even love.

This does not mean they are the Devil, but, he can speak through others to get to us. When we shut him down through them, then he attempts to speak directly to us in our own minds. Remember the Devil is a spirit and is desperate! Don't play with him, directly or indirectly… he is venomous and lethal if not checked!

We have been given all power over the enemy. Be wise as a serpent and don't replace prayer with production! Stop seeking things to entertain you when the Father desires to be intimate with you, give God his time. Be close to Him….PRAY!

* * *

Know this; the enemy was given permission, we've been given, AUTHORITY!

You don't need opinions concerning your time with your Lord. It's a personal relationship with Jesus. Know Him! Be with Him! Love on Him!

As He is the Resurrection and Life, He's able to Resurrect every dead thing in your life.

Establishing your relationship with the Lord will be your greatest asset and security for ever.

May the grace of our Lord Jesus Christ bless you continually. Be strong in the Lord. Keep the faith and hold Him dear to your hearts. What a glorious blessing for all who love God and His Son, manifestations through Holy Spirit?

Peace and joy, to my brothers and sisters of the kingdom. Love you!
If not here…I'll see you when we get Home.

Victory,

Your brother and Pastor Joseph Brice

Contents

* * *

CHAPTER ONE

B.C - A.D.

What does BC and AD mean?

BC and AD are the terms used to describe the years "Before Christ" (BC means before Christ) and "AD" (In the Year of Our Lord).

AD stands for the years after Jesus Christ was born. BC stands for the years before the birth of Christ. There is no year zero, so there is only the year 1 BC followed by AD 1.BC always comes after the year, and AD comes before the year.

What Year is BC and AD?

When we talk about the years BC, they go backward from year 0. So the BC years get bigger as you go to the left on a timeline.

The AD years go forward to the right.

Of course, our system of using BC notation didn't come about until centuries after the fact.

There's no way folks in those days could have known they were living in the days of having the years go backward!

In most everyday communication, we don't even use AD. We will just list the year as part of the date when we record day/month/year.

We use BC if we are talking about something that happened a really long time ago.

In normal conversation, it doesn't come up too much.

But you can't ignore the fact that the AD years started sometime. And there had to be a reason for it!

What does the Latin Phrase Anno Domini Mean?

Anno is a lot like our English word **Annual**, which denotes a year. Domini means **Lord (who dwells in dominion over all creation)** But AD is actually an abbreviation of the original term, which was quite a bit longer.The entire original Latin phrase is **"Anno Domini nostri Jesus"** which translates as "In the year of our Lord Jesus Christ."This explains why AD is regarded as meaning "In the year of our Lord." Some folks guess AD stands for "After Death."

But this meaning is impossible for AD. If it were true, there would be an approximate 33-year gap between BC and AD, which would be unworkable. Another thing to consider is the abundant and dramatic historical and literary evidence of Jesus' resurrection. Jesus' death is a very important historical fact.But the many overwhelming historical facts surrounding **his resurrection** make Jesus' factual return to life after a horrible death very compelling.It's interesting to note the Gregorian calendar and the AD notation are not essential to the Christian faith and are not part of Biblical teachings.BC and AD do not appear in the Bible. They do make it much easier to understand history, though!

So how did BC and AD happen?

The calendar we use today is a solar calendar.It's called the Gregorian calendar. It begins at the same place every year in the earth's orbit around the sun.It has become the world's standard calendar.But the calendar of the ancients was a lunar calendar based on the moon's orbit around the earth.

The Jewish calendar still in use today is a great example of a lunar calendar. So is the Chinese lunar calendar. This lunar system was fine in the early years of human history when everyone was looking forward. But in later years it made the historian's job difficult.There was no direct record of the years, so if a historian needed to calculate the date of some important event, it was very hard to do.And as western culture advanced, it became more important for commercial reasons to schedule events for future dates as well.

A change was in order, so an industrious Roman monk of Scythian origin named <u>Dionysius Exiguus</u> devised this new system in 525 AD.Dionysius had a great reputation for scholarship. He was known for making translations of many important works from Greek into Latin for the Pope.The then-current calendar system used data from the era of Diocletian. Dionysius didn't want to give glory to <u>Diocletian</u>, a bloodthirsty Roman Emperor who had brutally persecuted and murdered Christians.Dionysius did his work over 500 years after the birth of Christ and left no record of how he made the calculations.Later scholars found he was off by a few years, so the birth of Christ is currently listed as ~4-6 BC. Dionysius' small error is not a theological issue.

When Was AD First Used?

The birth of Christ remains the dividing line of world history just as he intended.It took several hundred years for Dionysius' work to catch on one nation at a time until the entire world accepted his calendar system.The first written records using this notation were by the English Priest Bede (Saint Venerable) who made numerous notations in 679, 692, 697, etc.

Why Do We Use BCE and CE?

[People Also Ask: "What is BC and AD now called?]

BCE stands for "Before the Common Era" (Before the Current Era) and CE stands for "Common Era" (Current Era) and both are substitutes for BC and AD. These terms date back to as early as the 18th Century.BCE and CE were popularized by people who were not Christians.They noted the very Christian nature of the BC and AD and that saying AD was acknowledging the Lordship of Jesus Christ.Not everybody is willing to do that, so the alternates allow them to use terms that seem more religiously neutral.

But it's apparent to all that there must be a reason for the divide, between BC and AD. And Christians can accept the usage of BCE and CE by unbelievers without taking offense.But the reason for this dividing line is the birth of Jesus Christ. There's just no avoiding it.We could easily say BCE and CE refer to "Before the Christian Era" and "Christian Era" since this dating system corresponds directly to the birth of Christ.

Birth Date of Jesus

In ancient times, the calendar began at the Regnal year one (first year of their reign) at the coronation (crowning) of every new monarch.So for example, we read about the history of the kings of Israel in the Old Testament, and there are references like this: "In the eighteenth year of King Jeroboam, Abijah began to reign over Judah." 2 Chronicles 13:1 The New Testament reads the same way "In the fifteenth year of the reign of Tiberius Caesar..." (Luke 3:1a, ESV)

So history began anew with the coronation of a new king.This is why we can pinpoint the birth of Christ down to a year. The Bible tells us the year in the terms of those days.The equivalent Hebrew year of Jesus' birth (~4 BC) would have been ~3756-3757.

When **Jesus Christ was born, he was immediately recognized as King** by the Magi. Now after Jesus was born in Bethlehem of Judea in the days of Herod the king, behold, wise men from the East came to

Jerusalem, saying, "Where is he who has been born **king of the Jews?** For we saw his star when it rose and have come to worship him." Matthew 2:1-2, ESV

Now we hear of the Magi and see the 3 men on camels in the nativity scenes and think it looks cute under the Christmas tree. But the Magi were powerful and influential men from a priestly caste of Persia who were not to be trifled with. The genealogy of Jesus would have been on scrolls in the temple so it was verifiable. And when the temple was destroyed in 70 AD, so were the genealogical records. So any later claim by another cannot be proven.

Jesus Christ remains King of the Jews (Matthew 27:37), and when he returns he will assert his kingship over the whole world. How appropriate then, that we mark the years since his birth as the years of his reign just as was done during ancient times for the earthly kings.

Jesus' birth lies at the horizontal intersection of world history. His death and resurrection lie at the vertical intersection of world history. This intersection of the horizontal and vertical are emblematic of his bridging the gap from man-to-man (Jesus is 100% man) and God-to-man (Jesus is 100% God).

If Jesus is not the Messiah, the Christ, why would the world who hated him agree to start time over in his honor? Especially those who do not believe. Where is Satan' power to stop this? Now you have those who are pushing the agenda to move related materials pointing to Jesus as the point of time and the Calder. How long did it take? Who was this person to cause such an upset in the world using love, peace, forgiveness, caring for the vulnerable and weak? He is the gift of God from Heaven—Emanuel, "God with us."

What will anyone say when they take their last breath and have to face this God? We do everything by the Calder and time. What will be your defense in the King's Court Room? Can your defense be you never heard of Jesus, or you never used time and a calendar? This man came as a modest working class carpenter or builder. He could have come as anything he chooses to but he came humble. He was rejected and despised.

Why would the Romans or any other being in power give this man such an honor who was accused, convicted and condemned to death by execution (crucifixion). There is so much evidence of Jesus being the manifested presence of God right here on earth among his people. God loves his people, the problem is, we need to love him back.

There are so many people who wish they could come back and do it all over again, but they blew it. Don't take the chance by not accepting the offering Jesus has afforded us. If you don't know him, start today. Repent, confess to him and take the rights that come with you as sons and daughters of the Most High God. One day we will all give an account for the life we have lived on this earth.

Good or evil we will be rewarded. We can submit and bow now or later. In his presence you will find how powerless you really are. People talk bad, but we will all witness how fear will grip them who are enemies of God, like no other experience before. Nothing can compare to the reality of facing your creator and having charges against you because you believed a Devil over God.

For it is written, As I live, saith the Lord, every knee shall bow to me, and every tongue shall confess to God. (Romans 14:11)

Wherefore God also hath highly exalted him, and given him a name which is above every name: that at the name of Jesus every knee should bow, of things in heaven, and things in earth, and things under the earth; and every tongue should confess that Jesus Christ is Lord, to the glory of God the Father. (Philippians 2: 99-11)

When you think about world history and timelines, God someway, somehow has always been in the picture. He is all knowing. The prophets and prophecies all line up, some took generations to come to pass. When we think of a God who resides in eternity while we are here in time, hundreds, thousands or even millions of years doesn't matter. He will get to what his plans are eventually. Even when people of power think they are fulfilling their own vision, someone placed it in the heart of that person.

For God has put in their hearts to fulfill his will, and to agree, and give their kingdom unto the beast, until the words of God shall be fulfilled. (Revelation 17: 17)

God put His imprint in this earth, especially through TIME! Second, minutes, hours, days, weeks, months and years...B.C.("Before Christ)" A.D. (Anno Domini, Latin phrase which means " in the year of our Lord.")

No matter how Satan tries to change it in these last days, it's TOO LATE, the world has already been saying and living "in the year of our Lord" like it or not...

CHAPTER TWO

Follow Me

"Follow Me"

Where did we first hear this? Is this new or is it a reoccurrence? We live in a world where it is very popular and a new normal through" Social Media" to follow someone. This generation is the most advance in technologies and access to what use to be impossible. To this generation God is granting access. Access to what—Secrets of HIs Kingdom? No other generations has seen more than this one. But, "To whom much is given, much is expected" (Luke 12:48). All of this knowledge seeking will have rewards or consequences.

Follow me, the informal invitation. Jesus is starting his ministry and goes to the Jordan River where John the Baptist is baptizing and preaching one message, " Repent for the kingdom of God is at hand." He is not bias or prejudice with his message... it's literally to everyone, until he encounters The One! Jesus leaves his job as a builder and is compelled to go and get baptized. It is his submission to his called and ultimate purpose. Jesus was working and holding down a job just like any one of us would today. But, something is calling him to his destiny...to his purpose for being in this world. He leaves his family, his job and heads on down to the Jordan River to be baptist of John.

Now John is at the Jordan preaching repentance and preparing for the coming of the One mightier than him. John is called the forerunner of Christ. Now who is John? John is the son of Zacharias and Elisabeth, both of the Tribe of Levi. Zacharias was a priest of the temple and Elisabeth was a daughter of

Aaron. Aaron of course was Moses's brother and the first established and ordained by God, to be a Priest of Israel...an Levitical Priest. John was conceived in his parents old age. Elisabeth was past the age of child bearing, John was their miracle baby. " For this is he that was spoken of by the prophet Isaiah, saying, "The voice of one crying in the wilderness, Prepare ye the way of the Lord, Make his paths straight" (Mathew 3:3) . "Behold, I will send you Elijah the prophet before the coming of the great and dreadful day of the LORD."" (Malachi 4:5)

John is sent for one purpose, and that is to prepare a people for the Lord. How is the preparation done? By way of repentance (to turn away from evil and return back to God). The first acknowledgment of sin or the separation from God is noted in the Bible in the Book of Genesis when Adam and Eve eats from the forbidden tree and its fruit, this caused the separation from God. Disobedience to God is the formula for separation. "For by one man's disobedience many were made sinners, so by the obedience of one shall many be made righteous" (Romans 5:19). All disobedience to God is sin. "Where in time past ye walked according to the course of this world, according to the prince of the power of the air, the spirit that now worth in the children of disobedience" (Ephesians 2:2).

John is gone! He is preaching a method unheard of, especially by his peers. He walked away from church, he left behind all natural riches and resources, most people don't realize how rich the Levitical Priest were. John came from a well to do family. No one could make heads or tails as to why John would go into the wilderness with nothing and live off the land, as a vagabond?

"And the same John had his clothing of camel's hair, and a leather belt about his waist; and his food was locusts and wild honey.(John 3:4)

Although the priest preached for 400 years since the prophet Malachi of the prophecy of one crying in the wilderness, when they see it, it's nothing as we imagined, though right there in our faces. It goes for truth even today. When someone comes along doing what preachers preach and teach about everyday, somehow, shuns the poor and seek the rich to hear.

John was sent to make the crooked way straight. John is considered to be the for runner to Jesus the Christ. Both of Jon's parents were very old when he was born, so I believe the losing of his parents was his sign to leave home, because there was nothing holding him there. He was the only child. John by revelation started preaching repentance and baptism. Many came to John and believed his message, but the Pharisees questioned him. They watched as the people followed John. They were wondering if in fact, he could be the Messiah, could he be the one? Because John was one of them, a Levite, a Priest, a descendant of Moses and Aaron, they were considering how to deal with John. John stage was the wilderness, totally exposed to the elements, no comfort and no shelter. His message was without prejudice and bias, across the board. *"Repent, for the kingdom of heaven is at hand (near)." This is he who was spoken of through the prophet Isaiah.*

"A voice of one crying in the wilderness, prepare the way for the Lord, make straight the pathway for him."

John's clothes were made of camel's hair, and he had a leather belt around his waist. His food was locusts and wild honey. People went out to him from Jerusalem and all Judea and the whole region of the Jordan. Confessing their sins, they were baptized by him in the Jordan River. But when he saw many of the Pharisees and Sadducees coming to where he was baptizing, he said to them: "You brood vipers! Who warned you to flee from the coming wrath? Produce fruit in keeping with repentance. And do not think you can say to yourselves, 'We have Abraham as our father.' I tell you that out of these stones God can raise up children for Abraham.

The ax is already at the root of the trees, and every tree that does not produce good fruit will be cut down and thrown into the fire. "I baptize you with water for repentance. But after me will come one who is more powerful than I, whose sandals I am not fit to carry. He will baptize you with the Holy Spirit and with fire. His winnowing fork is in his hand, and he will clear his threshing floor, gathering his wheat into the barn and burning up the chaff with unquenchable fire."

Then came Jesus from Galilee to Jordan unto John, to be baptized by him. But John forbad him, saying, I have need to be baptized by you, and come you to me? And Jesus answering said unto him, Let it to be so now: for it is proper for us to fulfill all righteousness." Then John consented. And as soon as Jesus, was baptized, he went up immediately out of the water: and, that moment the heavens were opened unto him, and he saw the Spirit of God descending like a dove, and lighting upon him: And lo a voice from heaven, saying, This is my beloved Son, in whom I am well pleased. (Mathew 3:4-17)

* * *

"Then Jesus was led by the Spirit into the wilderness to be tempted by the devil. The tempter came to him and said, "If you are the Son of God, tell these stones to become bread." Jesus answered, "It is written: 'Man shall not live on bread alone, but on every word that comes from the mouth of God.'" Then the devil took him to the holy city and had him stand on the highest point of the temple. "If you are the Son of God," he said, "throw yourself down.

For it is written: " 'He will command his angels concerning you, and they will lift you up in their hands, so that you will not strike your foot against a stone.'" Jesus answered him, "It is also written: 'Do not put the Lord your God to the test.'" Again, the devil took him to a very high mountain and showed him all the kingdoms of the world and their splendor. "All this I will give you," he said, "if you will bow down and worship me." Jesus said to him, "Away from me, Satan! For it is written: 'Worship the Lord, your God, and serve him only.'"Then the devil left him, and angels came and attended him."
(Matthew 4:1, 3-11)

Jesus by example shows us how the devil world when you answer your; calling. Rather than waiting on the devil to come and play with him through out his ministry, he went looking for him…now that's "Gangster!" Jesus knew Satan is the leader of his gang, and knows their capabilities, because in heaven they got their training and gifts from him. Jesus is the Word made flesh, so his words had empowered this fallen one.

*Note to the Five Fold ministers; if Jesus went to be tempted of the devil before he started his ministry, should we do as well? Everything the enemy will bring to him in his ministry, he made him expose it in the wilderness in private, before he did ministry in public. In other words, if you don't get the victory in private, the devil will not respect you in public.

This is the reason so many are afraid of the devil. They know that they took the offer from the devil in private, so how can they **rebuke** the devil in public. So they say things like this, "I don't even want to mention his name" or let's not talk about the devil, (most of the time…it's enemy) but Jesus called this devil out. Jesus took no bribes or prisoners.

Jesus turn down every offer the devil made. Remember when the devil showed him the kingdoms of the earth and their glory? This means, kingdoms of religion, government and world. The Pharisees were on the devil's payroll. Jesus saw it along with the world kingdoms.

Be sure Pastors and church leaders, that you didn't get your stuff you're calling blessings from the wrong source. Fact Check; Are you allowed to rebuke Satan? Do you have the authority to cast out devils? Can you say, "JESUS" without getting into trouble?

Jesus set people free, who wanted to be free, everywhere he went, cast out devils, embarrassed Satan and his demons. He showed his authority and power, over all the enemy.

"Jesus returned to Galilee in the power of the Spirit, and news about him spread through the whole countryside. He was teaching in their synagogues, and everyone praised him. He went to Nazareth, where he had been brought up, and on the Sabbath day he went into the synagogue, as was his custom. He stood up to read, and the scroll of the prophet Isaiah was handed to him.

Unrolling it, he found the place where it is written: "The Spirit of the Lord is on me, because he has anointed me to proclaim good news to the poor. He has sent me to proclaim freedom for the prisoners and recovery of sight for the blind, to set the oppressed free, to proclaim the year of the Lord's favor." Then he rolled up the scroll, gave it back to the attendant and sat down. The eyes of everyone in the synagogue were fastened on him.

He began by saying to them, "Today this scripture is fulfilled in your hearing." All spoke well of him and were amazed at the gracious words that came from his lips. "Isn't this Joseph's son?"they asked. Jesus said to them, "Surely you will quote this proverb to me: 'Physician, heal yourself!' And you will tell me, 'Do here in your hometown what we have heard that you did in Capernaum.'"

"Truly I tell you," he continued, "no prophet is accepted in his hometown. I assure you that there were many widows in Israel in Elijah's time, when the sky was shut for three and a half years and there was a severe famine throughout the land. Yet Elijah was not sent to any of them, but to a

widow in Zarephath in the region of Sidon. All the people in the synagogue were furious when they heard this.

They got up, drove him out of the town, and took him to the brow of the hill on which the town was built, in order to throw him off the cliff. But he walked right through the crowd and went on his way."
(Luke 4:14-26, 28-30)

Even Jesus couldn't do many mighty works there, because of their **unbelief!** Sometimes people are stuck with where and who you were before answering the calling. You will find, your most valuable time will have been wasted on people who are stuck in your past. Satan will use them to hold you hostage to the old you. It doesn't necessarily mean bad, just not converted for the calling and purposes of God. We go through processing before placement.

Although Jesus may have been an excellent builder, it was part of his process, not his destiny. So don't allow anyone to bound you to your process, go out to evaluate your progress. So you don't need more **ANOINTING, you need a different crowd. Don't change your message, change your audience!** Jesus preached the same message but got unprecedented results, because he was willing to leave his comfort zone. Even his family. Don't be afraid to change locations and people if necessary. If you do what God has called you to do, you may very well win your family later…but go!

"From that time on Jesus began to preach, "Repent, for the kingdom of heaven has come near." As Jesus was walking beside the Sea of Galilee, he saw two brothers, Simon called Peter and his brother Andrew. They were casting a net into the lake, for they were fishermen. "Come, follow me," Jesus said, "and I will send you out to fish for people." At once they left their nets and followed him.*

Going on from there, he saw two other brothers, James son of Zebedee and his brother John. They were in a boat with their father Zebedee, preparing their nets. Jesus called them, and immediately they left the boat and their father and followed him. Jesus went throughout Galilee, teaching in their synagogues, proclaiming the good news of the kingdom, and healing every disease and sickness among the people. News about him spread all over Syria, and people brought to him all who were ill with various diseases, those suffering severe pain, the demon-possessed, those having seizures, and the paralyzed; and he healed them.

Large crowds from Galilee, the Decapolis, Jerusalem, Judea and the region across the Jordan followed him."
(*Matthew 4:17-25*)

After this, Jesus and his disciples went out into the Judean countryside, where he spent some time with them, and baptized. Now John also was baptizing at Aenon near Salim, because there was plenty of water, and people were coming and being baptized. (This was before John was put in prison.)

An argument developed between some of John's disciples and a certain Jew over the matter of ceremonial washing. They came to John and said to him, "Rabbi, that man who was with you on the other side of the Jordan—the one you testified about—look, he is baptizing, and everyone is going to him."

To this John replied, "A person can receive only what is given them from heaven. You yourselves can testify that I said, 'I am not the Messiah but am sent ahead of him.' The bride belongs to the bridegroom. The friend who attends the bridegroom waits and listens for him, and is full of joy when he hears the bridegroom's voice. That joy is mine, and it is now complete.

He must become greater; I must become less." The one who comes from above is above all; the one who is from the earth belongs to the earth, and speaks as one from the earth. The one who comes from heaven is above all. He testifies to what he has seen and heard, but no one accepts his testimony. Whoever has accepted it has certified that God is truthful. For the one whom God has sent speaks the words of God, for God gives the Spirit without limit.

The Father loves the Son and has placed everything in his hands. Whoever believes in the Son has eternal life, but whoever rejects the Son will not see life, for God's wrath remains on them."
(*John 3:22-36 NIV*)

Look at how sly and messy the devil is, he had disciples thinking it was their idea to bring up the fact that the one John was on the other side baptizing. John spoke of Jesus the entire time he was baptizing. He even called Jesus, *"The Lamb of God, who comes to take away the sins of the world."*

The devil tried to start a competition between them two, and create strife. But see how John handled this situation. Unfortunately, today many of our leaders have not taken the precious jewels from these two leaders. This was the beginning of where we get the denominational divide. The devil would use this throughout the growth of the church.

The mission was to save, the purpose was to give birth to the church. Constantly, you will see followers go back and forth from followers of John and followers of Jesus. John baptized with water and Jesus later with fire. So as you read the book of acts, you will hear the effects of the followers representing their denomination.

The very beginning of the Baptist church verses the Pentecostal Church. They both preached repentance and the kingdom, and knew their purpose for being in this world. But, the devil continued to use weak people with hidden agendas, to bring division in the church, and it took a toll on the early church, and church to this day.

Some followers of John remained faithful, even after his death. They would proclaim themselves proudly as John's followers, while others broadly declared Jesus as Lord and asked if they had received the Holy Spirit? The church continued to grow tremendously, even while being persecuted! Jesus said, ***The gates of Hell will not prevail."***

These two leaders were of God and was pure at heart, and sent by God, but only one will prevail. Only Jesus is the Resurrection and the Life. The same devil who came after Jesus in the spirit, used people to continue to persecute the church, but could not stop her.

This is very important for us to understand, there is no competition in the kingdom. We unite to complete the vision, not cause division.

"At daybreak, Jesus went out to a solitary place. The people were looking for him and when they came to where he was, they tried to keep him from leaving them. But he said, "I must proclaim the good news of the kingdom of God to the other towns also, because that is why I was sent." And he kept on preaching in the synagogues of Judea."
(Luke 4:42-44)

* * *

The Cost of Discipleship

Jesus called his twelve disciples to him and gave them authority to drive out impure spirits and to heal every disease and sickness. These are the names of the twelve apostles: first, Simon (who is called Peter) and his brother Andrew; James son of Zebedee, and his brother John; Philip and Bartholomew; Thomas and Matthew the tax collector; James son of Alphaeus, and Thaddaeus; Simon the Zealot and Judas Iscariot, who betrayed him.

These twelve Jesus sent out with the following instructions: "Do not go among the Gentiles or enter any town of the Samaritans. Go rather to the lost sheep of Israel. As you go, proclaim this message: 'The kingdom of heaven has come near.' "Do not get any gold or silver or copper to take with you in your belts— no bag for the journey or extra shirt or sandals or a staff, for the worker is worth his keep.

Whatever town or village you enter, search there for some worthy person and stay at their house until you leave. As you enter the home, give it your greeting. If the home is deserving, let your peace rest on it; if it is not, let your peace return to you. If anyone will not welcome you or listen to your words, leave that home or town and shake the dust off your feet. Truly I tell you, it will be more bearable for Sodom and Gomorrah on the day of judgment than for that town.

"I am sending you out like sheep among wolves. Therefore be as shrewd as snakes and as innocent as doves. Be on your guard; you will be handed over to the local councils and be flogged in the synagogues. On my account you will be brought before governors and kings as witnesses to them and to the Gentiles. But when they arrest you, do not worry about what to say or how to say it. At that time you will be given what to say, for it will not be you speaking, but the Spirit of your Father speaking through you.

"Brother will betray brother to death, and a father his child; children will rebel against their parents and have them put to death. You will be hated by everyone because of me, but the one who stands firm to the end will be saved. When you are persecuted in one place, flee to another. Truly I tell you, you will not finish going through the towns of Israel before the Son of Man comes.

"The student is not above the teacher, nor a servant above his master. It is enough for students to be like their teachers, and servants like their masters.

If the head of the house has been called Beelzebul, how much more the members of his household! "So do not be afraid of them, for there is nothing concealed that will not be disclosed, or hidden that will not be made known.

Do not be afraid of those who kill the body but cannot kill the soul. Rather, be afraid of the One who can destroy both soul and body in hell. Are not two sparrows sold for a penny? Yet not one of them will fall to the ground outside your Father's care. And even the very hairs of your head are all numbered. "Whoever acknowledges me before others, I will also acknowledge before my Father in heaven.

"Do not suppose that I have come to bring peace to the earth. I did not come to bring peace, but a sword. For I have come to turn " 'a man against his father, a daughter against her mother, a daughter-in-law against her mother-in-law — a man's enemies will be the members of his own household.'

"Anyone who loves their father or mother more than me is not worthy of me; anyone who loves their son or daughter more than me is not worthy of me. Whoever does not take up their cross and follow me is not worthy of me. Whoever finds their life will lose it, and whoever loses their life for my sake will find it. "Anyone who welcomes you welcomes me, and anyone who welcomes me welcomes the one who sent me.

Whoever welcomes a prophet as a prophet will receive a prophet's reward, and whoever welcomes a righteous person as a righteous person will receive a righteous person's reward. And if anyone gives even a cup of cold water to one of these little ones who is my disciple, truly I tell you, that person will certainly not lose their reward."" (Matthew 10:1-7, 9-26, 28-30, 32, 34-42)

Jesus turned this world upside down with 12 men who new nothing about ministry and one of them was a devil. Don't be shock by your devil in your ministry. They are supposed to be there as a witness on the day of judgement, of how merciful God is, to even give the devil a chance to follow God and REPENT, but he just wouldn't, couldn't, maybe shouldn't, but is there for the ride, the money, glory and fame. Wanting to shine is costly! Don't let your devil hinder your destiny. When it's time to let them go...let them go!

"Then Jesus replied, "Have I not chosen you, the Twelve? Yet one of you is a devil!" (He meant Judas, the son of Simon Iscariot, who, though one

of the Twelve, was later to betray him.)"
  (John 6:70-71)

"As soon as Judas took the bread, Satan entered into him. So Jesus told him, "What you are about to do, do quickly.""
  (John 13:27)

Your Judas is there to remind you that the devil is close to you, not far away. Don't be afraid! That devil is close enough to you to kiss you but hates you and will sell you out in a heart beat for money! They study you, know you, testify against you, and convince sinners that you are a sinners, in hopes of destroying you. Don't REST but RISE! We have Resurrected Power! Keep it moving…

Stay focused! Judas will catapult you to your highest calling if you done quit, and or give him too much credit for being unified with Satan to destroy your purpose. He may get you hung, but he will hang him self, with no possible way of coming back. He went to church after he betrayed Jesus, and got paid (most think God is blessing them for them setting you up). Don't give too much attention to your Judas, it's just a matter of ***TIME! SO praise God, not your troubles caused by your betrayer, who was used by the devil. " What you must do…do it quickly!" Let's get it over with…I have work to do, after my crucifixion!***

The unbelievers constantly asked Jesus for a sign, Jesus said you will get no sign except for judgment. After all that Jesus had done, they still wanted to see signs. Wanting a performance…for what?

Many times we are so busy looking for signs and the coming of Jesus in the heavens, that we miss them right down here on earth. Our brothers and sisters who are in need, the great end time harvest. In the flesh (carnal) we see a bunch of poor people with needs and problems, but in the spirit realm, God sees His children and plenty of resources to take care of them. A great harvest ready to be picked and saved.

For I was hungry, and you gave me food: I was thirsty, and you gave me drink: I was a stranger, and you took me in: Naked, and you clothed me: I was sick, and you visited me: I was in prison, and you came unto me. Then shall the righteous answer him, saying, Lord, when saw we you hungry, and fed you? or thirsty, and gave you drink? When saw we you a stranger, and took you in? or naked, and clothed you? Or when saw we you sick, or in prison, and came unto you?

And the King shall answer and say unto them, Verily I say unto you, Since you have done it unto one of the least of these my brethren, you have done it unto me. (Mathew 25:35-40)

Follow Jesus!

Do you know Lucifer, the fallen one, copies everything that God touches. He's like the great counterfeit of what's real. The devil has no power or authority to giving you a life outside of this world. Everything he's bartering with, is stolen. He has deceived so many.

Do you know, "REPENTANCE" is what God chose as our way out. It is the equalizer. All who will do it, get's God's ear. John started a moment directed by God. Repentance is the way to the heart of God. If we repent, God forgives our sins and we get a clean slate. It doesn't matter what you've done. This is an act of Love, and Mercy.

Salvation was a plan…a divine plan. God worked out all the kinks. The devil and his children would rather argue the facts, rather than walking by faith and doing what God says. John said, "REPENT." Jesus came after John and preached, " REPENT" The kingdom of heaven is now within your reach. God came to us because we were too sinful to go to Him.

Jesus openly said, "Follow Me" think about our generation, social media is asking people to follow them, "Follow me." We must challenge ourselves after "chapter BC and AD" to this man called Jesus getting his ministry going without marketing and technology…just word of mouth…"Follow Me." He got two followers at a time. His ministry EXPLODED! It was like nothing ever done or seen before. He called twelve me to follow him and taught them, on the job, as they went.

Literally, Jesus did "On the job training." If Jesus turned the world upside down with "Follow Me" as the method and vehicle for his movement. This method was so unique and strategically put together, that when the church was under persecution, they could go from house to house to have service, worship and bible study teaching, hiding form their enemies. They couldn't worship as we do today and advertise, they had too many enemies and they still grew expeditiously.

Jesus taught his disciples how to be effective and powerful in growth by way of "Social" without the "media" but the start of a new movement and way to real people. They invited them to follow (in person or by sent message), friend request them, tag them and even block those who felt would be a threat to the movement. They were very discreet at times when it was necessary.

What was first, has been made last, and then first again. You don't think that in the end times, God would use what built the "First Church" to grow the "Last Church?" But this time Satan has had time to study the movement and plan as well as the, technology. The copycat and counterfeit is on it! Everything God does, the baby wants it too.

So Satan plans are to use everything to get his campaign moving. He's the Anti-Christ and he's sharpening his skills for this race. He's on a mission to be a thorn in the church's side. Bw careful, as to who you are following and who'd following you? Where are you being lead, and/or leading others to? Imagine on that day, God just pull all of our social media accounts as evidence for judgment. Are you ok with that? Would it be a problem?

The Beast is searching for his woman and his method! 666 is all around us, he's marketing his destruction camouflaged with beauty, excitement, feel goods all in trying times. One of the things prophesied was, people would be tired of all of the chaos and trouble and would become desperate for peace and safety, because of fears.

"The dragon stood on the shore of the sea. And I saw a beast coming out of the sea. It had ten horns and seven heads, with ten crowns on its horns, and on each head a blasphemous name. The beast I saw resembled a leopard, but had feet like those of a bear and a mouth like that of a lion.

The dragon gave the beast his power and his throne and great authority. One of the heads of the beast seemed to have had a fatal wound, but the fatal *wound had been healed. **The whole world was filled with wonder and followed the beast.** People worshiped the dragon because he had given authority to the beast, and they also worshiped the beast and asked, "**Who is like the beast?** Who can wage war against it?"*

*The beast was given a mouth to utter proud words and blasphemies and to exercise its authority for **forty-two months**. It opened its mouth to blaspheme God, and to slander his name and his dwelling place and those who live in heaven. It was given power to wage war against God's holy people and to conquer them. **And it was given authority over every tribe, people, language and nation.***

***All inhabitants of the earth will worship the beast—all whose names have not been written in the Lamb's book of life, the Lamb who was slain from the creation of the world.** Whoever has ears, let them hear. Because of the signs it was given power to perform on behalf of the first beast, it deceived the inhabitants of the earth. It ordered them to set up an image in honor of the beast who was wounded by the sword and yet lived.*

*The second beast was given power to give breath to the image of the first beast, so that the image could speak and cause all who refused to worship the image to be killed. It also forced all people, great and small, rich and poor, free and slave, to receive a mark on their right hands or on their foreheads, **so that they could not buy or sell unless they had the mark, which is the name of the beast or the number of its name. This calls for wisdom. Let the person who has insight calculate the number of the beast, for it is the number of a man. That number is 666.**" (Revelation 13:1-9, 14-18)*

How powerful is this? John was the disciple, turned apostle, and is said to be around 88 years old, at the time of these writings. He's on an island and Jesus appears to him and tells John to write what he sees. Jesus is revealing to him futuristic events. They are not making since to John, on the account he's seeing the future and trying to describe what he sees.

Remember when ,*"Jesus said this to indicate the kind of death by which Peter would glorify God. Then he said to him, "**Follow me!**" Peter turned and saw that the disciple whom Jesus loved was following them. (This was the one who had leaned back against Jesus at the supper and had said, "Lord, who is going to betray you?")*

* * *

When Peter saw him, he asked, "Lord, what about him?" Jesus answered, "If I want him to remain alive until I return, what is that to you? **You must follow me.** *" Because of this, the rumor spread among the believers that this disciple would not die. But Jesus did not say that he would not die; he only said, "If I want him to remain alive until I return, what is that to you?"*

This is the disciple who testifies to these things and who wrote them down. We know that his testimony is true. Jesus did many other things as well. If every one of them were written down, I suppose that even the whole world would not have room for the books that would be written." (John 21:19-25)

"Then said Jesus unto his disciples, If any man will come after me, let him deny himself, and take up his cross, and **follow me.** *For whosoever will save his life shall lose it: and whosoever will lose his life for my sake shall find it. For what is a man profited, if he shall gain the whole world, and lose his own soul?*

Or what shall a man give in exchange for his soul? For the Son of man shall come in the glory of his Father with his angels; and then he shall reward every man according to his works. Verily I say unto you, There be some standing here, which shall not taste of death, till they see the Son of man coming in his kingdom."(Matthew 16:24-28 KJV)

"Until I return" this man saw Jesus and was the last one standing of those who were there that day as witnesses to this account. But what's much more amazing to me is, John loved Jesus so much and was the youngest disciple of the twelve. By seeking God, loving God and spending time devoted to God, he revealed many of heaven's secrets to John.

So young people don't let anyone deter you from seek God, he is not a bore. Don't let anyone tell you that you can't visit God or have heavenly experiences before you go there…or should I say, go home.

Be sure to know who you are **following** and what you are following. Be accountable, because one day you will be asked to give an account for the gifts you were given in life. **GREAT IS YOUR REWARD!**

* * *

Be sure to lead people to the light and life. **"Only follow me, if I am following Christ!"**

Jesus is the originator of, "FOLLOW ME."

CHAPTER THREE

Passover

"Nothing but the BLOOD!"

"I Know It Was The Blood That Saved Me"

Passover, or Pesach in Hebrew, is one of the Jewish religion's most sacred and widely observed holidays. In Judaism, Passover commemorates the story of the Israelites' departure from ancient Egypt, which appears in the Hebrew Bible's books of Exodus, Numbers, and Deuteronomy, among other texts. Jews observe the week-long festival with a number of important rituals, including a traditional Passover meal known as a seder, the removal of leavened products from their home, the substitution of matzo for bread and the retelling of the exodus.

According to the Hebrew Bible, Jewish settlement in ancient Egypt first occurs when Joseph, a son of the patriarch Jacob and founder of one of the 12 tribes of Israel, moves his family there during a severe famine in their homeland of Canaan. For many years the Israelites live in harmony in the province of Goshen, but as their population grows the Egyptians begin to see them as a threat. After the death of Joseph and his brothers, the story goes, a particularly hostile pharaoh orders their enslavement and the systematic drowning of their firstborn sons in the Nile.

One of these doomed infants is rescued by the pharaoh's daughter, given the name Moses (meaning "one who is pulled out") and adopted into the Egyptian royal family.

When he reaches adulthood, Moses becomes aware of his true

identity and the Egyptians' brutal treatment of his fellow Hebrews. He kills an Egyptian slave master and escapes to the Sinai Peninsula, where he lives as a humble shepherd for forty years. One day, however, Moses receives a command from God to return to Egypt and free his kin from bondage, according to the Hebrew bible. Along with his brother Aaron, Moses approaches the reigning pharaoh (who is unnamed in the biblical version of the story) several times, explaining that the Hebrew God has requested a three-day leave for his people so that they may celebrate a feast in the wilderness.

When the pharaoh refuses, God unleashes 10 plagues on the Egyptians, including turning the Nile River red with blood, diseased livestock, boils, hailstorms and three days of darkness, culminating in the slaying of every firstborn son by an avenging angel. The Israelites, however, mark the door frames of their homes with lamb's blood so that the angel of death will recognize and "pass over" each Jewish household. Terrified of further punishment, the Egyptians convince, their ruler to release the Israelites, and Moses quickly leads them out of Egypt. The pharaoh changes his mind, however, and sends his soldiers to retrieve the former slaves.

As the Egyptian army approaches the fleeing Jews at the edge of the Red Sea, a miracle occurs: God causes the sea to part, allowing Moses and his followers to cross safely, then closes the passage and drowns the Egyptians. According to the Hebrew Bible, the Jews—now numbering in the hundreds of thousands—then trek through the Sinai desert for 40 tumultuous years before finally reaching their ancestral home in Canaan, later known as the Land of Israel.

One of the most important Passover rituals for observant Jews is removing all leavened food products (known as Chametz) from their home before the holiday begins and abstaining from them throughout its duration. Instead of bread, religious Jews eat a type of flatbread called matzo. According to tradition, this is because the Hebrews fled Egypt in such haste that there was no time for their bread to rise.

Passover also distinguishes itself from other Jewish holidays because it's a holiday primarily celebrated in the home, rather than at synagogue. This can make the holiday feel more like Thanksgiving than like a traditional, dress-up-and-go-to-services holiday. It also means that individual families have a lot of leeway to create and maintain their own Passover traditions. It's extremely unlikely that any two Seders you go to, will be identical.

Judaism is a religion of remembering, and the tradition of

Passover is a great example of how the concept of memory preservation works in Judaism. The story of Passover includes multiple occasions of God protecting the Hebrews because he remembers the promise he has made to them. Passover, then, is the time when Jews remember that God remembered them.

Why was Jesus in Jerusalem? Scriptures shared by Jews and Christians demand that three times a year the faithful are to celebrate festivals in Jerusalem (Exodus 23:14; 2Chronicles 8:13); they are the feasts of Passover (Unleavened Bread), Weeks (Shavuot), and Booths (Tabernacles or Sukkot). The three are the appointed feasts listed in Leviticus 23:2 (compare 2 Chronicles 31:3; Ezra 3:5). Jerusalem, Zion, is the city of the feasts, as noted in Isaiah 33:20. The most important festival was Passover.

Jesus was devoutly Jewish. According to Luke (2:41–42), Jesus's family went to Jerusalem every year at Passover, and when Jesus was 12, his parents went to the Temple, perhaps for his Bar Mitzvah (conceivably his cousin, John, was present). According to sacred traditions, God demanded that all males appear in Jerusalem to celebrate Passover (Exodus 23:17; Deuteronomy 16:16). All must recline to dine, an arrangement that is clear in Jesus's Last Supper according to John 13:23.

According to Mark (14:12–21), Matthew (26:17–25), Luke (22:7–14, 21–23), and John (13:21–30), Jesus was in Jerusalem to celebrate Passover. The first three gospels describe the first day of Passover, when approximately 10,000 lambs were slaughtered in the Temple, Jesus's disciples prepared the Passover meal in the upper room of a house in southwest Jerusalem. Jesus's last supper was either the Passover meal (according to Matthew, Mark and Luke) or a meal just before Passover with Passover traditions informing the evening (John). Following customs that are now well over 2,000 years old, Jesus broke bread, raised the cup full of wine, and chanted the Passover hymn. If Jesus broke "leavened bread," then it was not matzah and it could not be a Passover meal. Mark (14:26) adds that, "When they had sung the hymn, they went out to the Mount of Olives."

Why was that Week important? The annual pilgrimage to Jerusalem is the time in the Spring, when Jews celebrate God's formation of Israel when he delivered the nation from slavery in Egypt. The annual celebration is shaped by a shared memory of that deliverance and a focus on experiencing anew God's pivotal miracle. Passover continued for seven days (Exodus 12:15; Leviticus 23:6), beginning on the fourteenth of the first month in the evening. The paschal lamb was eaten on the first evening (Exodus 12:6, 8).

Long before Jesus, Jewish traditions reflected a long, sacred commemoration of Passover each year. For example, those with Moses left the city of Rameses in Egypt the day after the initial Passover. According to Joshua (5:10) Israelites celebrated Passover at Gilgal, while King Josiah celebrated the Passover in Jerusalem (2 Chronicles 35:1,16). And those returning from the Babylonian exile celebrated the Passover (Ezra 6:19). Knowing these ancient traditions helps us appreciate Jesus's wish: "I have eagerly desired to eat this Passover with you" (Luke 22:15).

The traditions in the Passover Haggadah (literally "The Telling of the Passover Story") antedate Jesus. It is a "scroll," or book, Jews read the first night of Passover to commemorate "the Season of our freedom in love, a holy convocation, commemorating the departure from Egypt." As the wine cup is raised, Jews bless "the LORD, our God, King of the universe."

Within a few decades of Jesus's Passover, Paul coined the concept that, "Christ our paschal lamb has been sacrificed." He urged Jesus's followers to continue to celebrate Passover: "let us celebrate the feast, (but) not with the old leaven of malice and evil" (1 Corinthians 5:7–8).

Paul seems to know the Passover Haggadah. First, in 1Corinthians 10:4, Paul implies that the rock followed after the Hebrews in their wanderings; according to the Passover Haggadah, the rock was round. Having rolled itself up like a swarm of bees, it followed the Hebrews. Paul helps with a metaphorical meaning by adding that it is "the spiritual rock that followed them." Second, in 1 Corinthians 10:16, in the celebration of Passover, Paul mentions "the cup of blessing;" those exact words are said by the leader of the seder.

Thus, Jesus's Last Supper becomes "the Lord's Supper," the Eucharist. Fluid traditions swirled in the minds of Jesus's first followers as the Exodus from Egypt framed the life and exodus of Jesus.

Today, Jews celebrate Passover (in Jesus's language); many look for the coming of the Messiah. Christians celebrate Passover as Easter. Many remember that the Messiah has come, and memorize words like these (in over one hundred languages): "On the evening of Jesus's last supper, he took bread. Giving thanks, he said this is my body, as you eat it, remember me. After supper, Jesus took a chalice and said, drink this wine in memory of me."

In Jerusalem today, Jews and Christians gather around a table, with their respective families, and celebrate a very old festival in the breaking of bread and drinking of wine. Memory flavors life with meaning; two groups remember God's mighty Salvific works, with words pregnant with a kaleidoscope of meanings: "And out of Egypt I called my son" (Hosea 11:1).

A one-year-old unblemished male lamb is chosen for the Passover by a member of the household. (In A. D. 33, Nisan 10 fell on 'Palm Monday,' the day Jesus made his triumphal entry into Jerusalem. It is evident that he was presenting himself as the unblemished sacrifice for the nation on that day.) The slaughter of the lambs would not take place until Nisan 14, the day Jesus was crucified (Friday, April 3, A. D. 33).

Usually the evening before the Passover meal was eaten, the *paterfamilias* led his family through the house by candlelight, looking in nooks and crannies for any leaven in the house. No leaven was supposed to be in the home at that time. (Not infrequently, Jews would sell their leaven to their Gentile neighbors and buy it back after the eight days of unleavened bread!)

As guests and family members entered the home to celebrate Passover, a servant or slave would often be there to wash their feet. This was the task of the lowest class of people. (That Jesus did this in (John 13), even though he was the paterfamilias or head of the family, both symbolizes what he would later do for his disciples [cf. Mark 10:45—"The Son of man did not come to be served, but to serve, and to give my life as a ransom for many"] and embodies his principle that "If anyone wants to be first, he shall be last of all, and servant of all" [Mark 9:35; cf. also John 13:15].)
"Blessed are you, O Lord our God, king of the universe, who has created the fruit of the vine..."

"Blessed are you, O Lord our God, King of the Universe who brings forth bread from the earth. Blessed are you, O Lord our God, King of the universe, who has sanctified us with your commandments, and commanded us to eat unleavened bread."

The host breaks the guest of honor's bread and they dip it together in the *Charoseth* and bitter herbs. The guest in turn breaks his neighbor's bread and they dip it together, and so on down the line.

"The name of the Lord be blessed from now until eternity. Let us bless him of whose gifts we have partaken: Blessed be our God of whose gifts we have partaken, and by whose goodness we exist."

"Blessed are you, O Lord our God, king of the universe, who has created the fruit of the vine. . .

"**I will redeem** you with an outstretched arm and with great judgments."

"Then **I will take** you as my people, and I will be your God; and you shall know that I am the Lord Your, God who brought you out from under the burdens of the Egyptians."

Passover lambs were slain between noon and 3 p.m. , there were three hours of darkness, from approximately noon to 3 p.m., when Jesus was on the cross [Mark 15:33]. When Jesus died, the temple curtain was torn in two, from top to bottom [Mark 15:38]—right when the last of the lambs would be on the altar in front of the sanctuary!). In A. D. 70, the last year that the temple was still standing, 270,000 lambs were slain.

When the lambs were slain, the Levites would chant the Psalms (Psalms 113-118) repeatedly.

This practice apparently stems from a rabbinic interpretation of Zephaniah 1:12—"I will search Jerusalem with lamps and punish those who are complacent.'" Since leaven often represents sin, Paul makes the tie between the leaven of the Passover and our commitment to Christ in 1 Cor. 5:7 ("Get rid of the old leaven that you may be a new batch without leaven—as you really are. For Christ, our Passover lamb, has been sacrificed.")

Jesus was that Passover Lamb and still is, The Lamb of God who take away the sins of the world.

I asked a friend of mine who is a Jew (Israelite) do you accept Jesus as the Messiah, The Passover Lamb prophesied to come? He said, "No way!" I asked, " Why Not?" "Because the Messiah has not come yet," he said. I asked, "What evidence do you have to support that theory?" He responded, "According to the Law of Moses.

So I asked, "Do you guys still bring your lambs without mark or blemish for the atonement for you and your family's sins for the year?" "No, he said." Then I asked, "Why not? If Jesus is not the Messiah, Son of God and Lamb of God, sent by God to fulfill prophecy, then who was he? ...And why are you guys not bring you lams or sheep to the Passover to be sacrificed for the atonement of your sins as a people?"

This is the Law of Moses in-which still is in effect. " HE said, he would ask his priest and get back to me. Well, he did, in a very timely matter and I was impressed. Excited, I was very eager to hear the answer, being that I'm not Jewish, I was thinking, maybe I have missed something? My friend said, "His priest would get back to him, after he reach out to someone in Israel." Long story short, they had no answer for me, in my case…**Jesus is the Answer**.

According to the Levitical Law, a sacrificed of sheep or goats were required of each family, or household for the atonement of their sins. The animal was slayed as the living sacrifice (alter) and blood was put in a bowl for the person or family for the atonement of their sins. At Passover the requirement was to bring your very best offering (lamb/sheep) without spot or blemish—perfect.

Your offering is taken behind the veil and slayed pouring the blood into a bowl and then brought out to perform the ritual or tradition of the sins being removed from the person and/or persons that the sacrificed was presented. This atonement for the sins committed was beloved to have been removed and cover then until next passover with would be for a year. Passover is a 7 day (Holy Week) celebration and service to the people.

Jesus was at Passover week and is noted of his triumphal entry into Jerusalem on a donkey.   This is widely seen as a recapitulation of the enthronement of Solomon (described in 1 Kings: 1) where at King David's direction, *he is anointed as king, at the Gihon Spring and rides his father's donkey into the city to the acclaim of the people. When Jesus rode into the Jerusalem on a donkey,* the Jews what it meant. The shouted out,"Hosanna, Hosanna!

"On the next day much people that were come to the feast, when they heard that Jesus was coming to Jerusalem, took branches of palm trees, and went forth to meet him, and cried, Hosanna: Blessed is the King of Israel that cometh in the name of the Lord. And Jesus, when he had found a young ass, sat thereon; as it is written, Fear not, daughter of Sion: behold, thy King cometh, sitting on an ass's colt.

These things understood not his disciples at the first: but when Jesus was glorified, then remembered they that these things were written of him, and that they had done these things unto him. The people therefore that was with him when he called Lazarus out of his grave, and raised him from the dead, bare record.

* * *

For this cause the people also met him, for that they heard that he had done this miracle. The Pharisees therefore said among themselves, Perceive ye how ye prevail nothing? Behold, the world is gone after him."
John 12:12-19 KJV

When King David was very old, he wanted to established his favored son Solomon as his successor. So he arranged for Solomon to ride on David's own mule, in the company of Zadok the priest and Nathan the prophet. By entering the city on a donkey Jesus to the Pharisees and priests, was his self proclaim as king (Jesus is noted as being; Prophet, Priest and King), they couldn't see that and neither were they trying to. Jesus was from Nazareth, that was enough to fuel the fire of the Pharisees (Tribe of Levy) , they were the elite group (Levites) of all the tribes of Israel…rich and dignified.

Jesus also is referred to as, The Son of David, *"The book of the generation of Jesus Christ, the son of David, the son of Abraham (Mathew 1:1) , And all the people were amazed, and said, Is this not the son of David (Mathew 12:23), While the Pharisees were gathered together, Jesus asked them, Saying, What think you of Christ? whose son is he? They say to him, The son of David (Mathew 22:41,42),*

And, behold, two blind men sitting by the way side, when they heard that Jesus passed by, cried out, saying, Have mercy on us, O, Lord, you son of David. And the multitude rebuked them, because they should hold their Peace: but they cried the more, saying, Have mercy on us, O, Lord, you son of David. And Jesus stood still, and called them, and said, What will you that I shall do to you? They say to him, Lord, that our eyes may be opened. So Jesus had compassion on them, and touched their eyes: and immediately their eyes received sight, and they followed him (Mathew 20:30-34).

Much people of the Jews therefore knew that he was there: and they came not for Jesus' sake only, but that they might see Lazarus also, whom he had raised from the dead. But the chief priests consulted that they might put Lazarus also to death; Because that by reason of him many of the Jews went away, and believed on Jesus. On the next day much people that were come to the feast, **when they heard that Jesus was coming to Jerusalem, Took branches of palm trees, and went forth to meet him, and cried, Hosanna: Blessed is the King of Israel that comes in the name of the Lord. This is where we get, "Palm Sunday."**

And Jesus, when he had found a young ass, sat thereon; as it is written,

Fear not, daughter of Sion: behold, your King comes, sitting on an ass's colt. These things understood not his disciples at the first: but when Jesus was glorified, then remembered they that these things were written of him, and that they had done these things to him. The people therefore that was with him when he called Lazarus out of his grave, and raised him from the dead, bore record. For this cause the people also met him, for that they heard that he had done this miracle. The Pharisees therefore said among themselves, Perceive you how you prevail nothing? Behold, the world is gone after him. (John 12:9-19)(KJV)

Now the first day of the feast of unleavened bread the disciples came to Jesus, saying unto him, Where wilt thou that we prepare for thee to eat the passover? And he said, Go into the city to such a man, and say unto him, The Master saith, My time is at hand; I will keep the passover at thy house with my disciples. And the disciples did as Jesus had appointed them; and they made ready the passover.

Now when the even was come, he sat down with the twelve. And as they did eat, he said, Verily I say unto you, that one of you shall betray me. And they were exceeding sorrowful, and began every one of them to say unto him, Lord, is it I? And he answered and said, He that dips his hand with me in the dish, the same shall betray me. The Son of man goeth as it is written of him: but woe unto that man by whom the Son of man is betrayed! it had been good for that man if he had not been born. Then Judas, which betrayed him, answered and said, Master, is it I?

He said unto him, Thou hast said and as they were eating, Jesus took bread, and blessed it, and brake it, and gave it to the disciples, and said, Take, eat; this is my body. And he took the cup, and gave thanks, and gave it to them, saying, Drink ye all of it; For this is my blood of the new testament, which is shed for many for the remission of sins. But I say unto you, I will not drink henceforth of this fruit of the vine, until that day when I drink it new with you in my Father's kingdom.

And when they had sung an hymn, they went out into the mount of Olives. Then saith Jesus unto them, All ye shall be offended because of me this night: for it is written, I will smite the shepherd, and the sheep of the flock shall be scattered abroad. But after I am risen again, I will go before you into Galilee.
(Mathew 26:17-32)

* * *

Jesus broke himself at that Passover Feast as the Lamb of God, this is why at the cross they couldn't break his legs. For these things were done, that the scripture should be fulfilled, "*A bone of him shall not be broken. And again another scripture saith, They shall look on him whom they pierced.* (John 19:36-37)

Jesus established the new "Kingdom Order" and standard for Passover. To this day very at Passover is celebrated and observed globally and wine and bread are used, there is no other form of lamb or blood sacrifice. Why do we fight the truth of God? If Jesus (Yeshua, Messiah) is not the Lamb of God…then who is?

The next day John sees Jesus coming unto him, and saith, Behold the Lamb of God, which taketh away the sin of the world. This is he of whom I said, After me cometh a man which is preferred before me: for he was before me. And I knew him not: but that he should be made manifest to Israel, therefore am I come baptizing with water. And John bare record, saying, I saw the Spirit descending from heaven like a dove, and it abode upon him.

And I knew him not: but he that sent me to baptize with water, the same said unto me, Upon whom thou shalt see the Spirit descending, and remaining on him, the same is he which baptizes with the Holy Ghost. And I saw, and bare record that this is the Son of God.

Again the next day after John stood, and two of his disciples; And looking upon Jesus as he walked, he saith, Behold the Lamb of God! (John 1:29-36)

And I saw in the right hand of him that sat on the throne a book written within and on the backside, sealed with seven seals. And I saw a strong angel proclaiming with a loud voice, Who is worthy to open the book, and to loose the seals thereof? And no man in heaven, nor in earth, neither under the earth, was able to open the book, neither to look thereon.

And I wept much, because no man was found worthy to open and to read the book, neither to look thereon. And one of the elders saith unto me, Weep not: behold, the Lion of the tribe of Juda, the Root of David, hath prevailed to open the book, and to loose the seven seals thereof. And I beheld, and, lo, in the midst of the throne and of the four beasts, and in the midst of the elders, stood a Lamb as it had been slain, having seven horns and seven eyes, which are the seven Spirits of God sent forth into all the earth. And he came and took the book out of the right hand of him that sat upon the throne.

And when he had taken the book, the four beasts and four and twenty elders fell down before the Lamb, having every one of them harps, and golden vials full of odors, which are the prayers of saints. And they sung a new song, saying, Thou art worthy to take the book, and to open the seals thereof: for thou wast slain, and hast redeemed us to God by thy blood out of every kindred, and tongue, and people, and nation; And hast made us unto our God kings and priests: and we shall reign on the earth.

And I beheld, and I heard the voice of many angels round about the throne and the beasts and the elders: and the number of them was ten thousand times ten thousand, and thousands of thousands; Saying with a loud voice, Worthy is the Lamb that was slain to receive power, and riches, and wisdom, and strength, and honor, and glory, and blessing.

And every creature which is in heaven, and on the earth, and under the earth, and such as are in the sea, and all that are in them, heard I saying, Blessing, and honor, and glory, and power, be unto him that sits upon the throne, and unto the Lamb for ever and ever.
And the four beasts said, Amen. And the four and twenty elders fell down and worshipped him that liveth for ever and ever. (Revelation Chapter 5)

All the evidence points to Jesus as the fulfillment of the Old Testament prophesies, (types and shadows of what's to come—the **real**). He is the Passover! He is the Lamb of God! He is the Son of God, He was and is the last needed and sacrifice and burnt offering, accepted by God! The religious leaders burned him, betrayed him, hated him, killed him, tried to annihilate him, but you cannot get rid of God, neither in time or eternity. Lucifer-Satan-the Devil has already tried, on many attempts. This is why his death was so barbaric and brutal, it was a *"Hate Crime!"*

The Blood of Christ

"But when Christ came as high priest of the good things that are now already here, he went through the greater and more perfect tabernacle that is not made with human hands, that is to say, is not a part of this creation. He did not enter by means of the blood of goats and calves; but he entered the Most Holy Place once for all by his own blood, thus obtaining eternal

redemption.

The blood of goats and bulls and the ashes of a heifer sprinkled on those who are ceremonially unclean sanctify them so that they are outwardly clean. How much more, then, will the blood of Christ, who through the eternal Spirit offered himself unblemished to God, cleanse our consciences from acts that lead to death, so that we may serve the living God! For this reason Christ is the mediator of a new covenant, that those who are called may receive the promised eternal inheritance—now that he has died as a ransom to set them free from the sins committed under the first covenant. In the case of a will, it is necessary to prove the death of the one who made it, This is why even the first covenant was not put into effect without blood.

When Moses had proclaimed every command of the law to all the people, he took the blood of calves, together with water, scarlet wool and branches of hyssop, and sprinkled the scroll and all the people. He said, "This is the blood of the covenant, which God has commanded you to keep." In the same way, he sprinkled with the blood both the tabernacle and everything used in its ceremonies. In fact, the law requires that nearly everything be cleansed with blood, and without the shedding of blood there is no forgiveness.

It was necessary, then, for the copies of the heavenly things to be purified with these sacrifices, but the heavenly things themselves with better sacrifices than these. For Christ did not enter a sanctuary made with human hands that was only a copy of the true one; he entered heaven itself, now to appear for us in God's presence. Nor did he enter heaven to offer himself again and again, the way the high priest enters the Most Holy Place every year with blood that is not his own.

Otherwise Christ would have had to suffer many times since the creation of the world. But he has appeared once for all at the culmination of the ages to do away with sin by the sacrifice of himself. Just as people are destined to die once, and after that to face judgment, so Christ was sacrificed once to take away the sins of many; and he will appear a second time, not to bear sin, but to bring salvation to those who are waiting for him."Hebrews 9:11-16, 18-28 NIV

They continued to offer up blood from sheep and lambs long after Jesus was crucified.   Stubborn and religious were they....Where are they now?

CHAPTER FOUR

The Cross

Jesus Didn't Just Died For You, But Died As You, So You Can Become Him, As He Became You...

Jesus came and died as the second man and last man Adam, to give us our place back with God. Reconciled and restored back to our place in God. We must in turn receive what he's done and die to the Adam concept, the curse has been nailed to the CROSS, and my blessed life came out the grave with Jesus, who is now sitting in heavenly places, lifting me up beside him, calling me blessed! RISE UP PEOPLE OF GOD...RISE UP!

As difficult and challenging it was, Jesus went to that cross! It wasn't easy at all. We see the decorated versions of the cross and in some regards, miss the point of pain and sacrifice. Why would someone sacrifice their life and submit to such disgrace and shame?

"For God so loved the world, that he gave his only begotten Son, that whosoever believes in him should not perish, but have everlasting life. For God sent not his Son into the world to condemn the world; but that the world through him might be saved." (John 3:16-17 KJV)

The Suffering Servant,

"Who has believed our message and to whom has the arm of the Lord been revealed? He grew up before him like a tender shoot, and like a root out of

dry ground. He had no beauty or majesty to attract us to him, nothing in his appearance that we should desire him. He was despised and rejected by mankind, a man of suffering, and familiar with pain. Like one from whom people hide their faces he was despised, and we held him in low esteem.

Surely he took up our pain and bore our suffering, yet we considered him punished by God, stricken by him, and afflicted. But he was pierced for our transgressions, he was crushed for our iniquities; the punishment that brought us peace was on him, and by his wounds we are healed. We all, like sheep, have gone astray, each of us has turned to our own way; and the Lord has laid on him the iniquity of us all.

He was oppressed and afflicted, yet he did not open his mouth; he was led like a lamb to the slaughter, and as a sheep before its shearers is silent, so he did not open his mouth. By oppression and judgment he was taken away. Yet who of his generation protested? For he was cut off from the land of the living; for the transgression of my people he was punished.

He was assigned a grave with the wicked, and with the rich in his death, though he had done no violence, nor was any deceit in his mouth. Yet it was the Lord's will to crush him and cause him to suffer, and though the Lord makes his life an offering for sin, he will see his offspring and prolong his days, and the will of the Lord will prosper in his hand.

After he has suffered, he will see the light of life and be satisfied; by his knowledge my righteous servant will justify many, and he will bear their iniquities. Therefore I will give him a portion among the great, and he will divide the spoils with the strong, because he poured out his life unto death, and was numbered with the transgressors. For he bore the sin of many, and made intercession for the transgressors."
Isaiah 53:1-12 NIV

The Cross

We are saved by what Jesus did at the cross, on the cross. No matter what the enemy thought he was doing, God is in control, the cross was his divine plan. His death was a reflection of how much much Lucifer's hate for God. He was jealous…so jealous. Get this, it is the first time, the devil gets his hour to put his hands on God for the first time ever, without security, or restrictions. The devil knew the angels were present, but forbidden to make a move. Satan is not that powerful. God tied his own hands to give Satan confidence that nothing would happen to him, so, express yourself. The brutality of the death of our Lord Jesus Christ, was the enemy's very true heart expressed. This enemy hates our God! God never died before, and now what's gonna happen. Satan putting his hands on God was the greatest high he ever had, but like all drugs, they can't last forever, but his heart was put on public display. Now the angels got to see the truth God had to them. Lucifer hated me even when he was here in the family. He didn't show it, like a person planning a murder. A lying cheating spouse, who think you don't no they are cheating. Lucifer thought he was getting away with his hypocrisy.

"Then he called the crowd to him along with his disciples and said: "Whoever wants to be my disciple must deny themselves and take up their cross and follow me." (Mark 8:34 NIV)

"For the message of the cross is foolishness to those who are perishing, but to us who are being saved it is the power of God." (1 Corinthians 1:18 NIV)

"For the message of the cross is foolishness to those who are perishing, but to us who are being saved it is the power of God."
  1 Corinthians 1:18 NIV

The cross was brutal, bloody, evil, painful and absolutely necessary, the very exact expression of the devil's hate for God. Love brought God to this world and hate took him out!

It was the **cross** that God used to save us! It was the hardest thing God has ever done according to records. We should take it lightly what he's done for us. How would anyone be able to stand before Jesus and ignore the pain and suffering.

"Therefore, since we are surrounded by such a great cloud of witnesses, let us throw off everything that hinders and the sin that so easily entangles. And let us run with perseverance the race marked out for us, fixing our eyes on Jesus, the pioneer and perfecter of faith. For the joy set before him he endured the cross, scorning its shame, and sat down at the right hand of the throne of God. Consider him who endured such opposition from sinners, so that you will not grow weary and lose heart." (Hebrews 12:1-3 NIV)

"But God demonstrates his own love for us in this: While we were still sinners, Christ died for us."
  Romans 5:8 NIV

Religion without the presence of God is lethal. It is so sad how people can dedicate their entire lives to a religion and not have a clue as to who God is. The Pharisees represented the elite and masters of the word of God, in their time. No on was considered as influential and astute as the Pharisees and Sadducees. They knew God's word, like the back of their hands, but yet , even still, they did not know God as well as they thought.

They fought the will of God every step of the way of fulfillment of the prophecies. To the people, they were as close as you get to God, until God shows up. This is a good place to observe and evaluation. Let's take a look at how far off the leaders of the church were, and how they handled the same God in-home they taught and preached every week about.   Sometimes we can do something for so long, we don't even realize we've loss sight as to why we even do what we do...we're just doing it. What's the point, and better yet, what's the purpose?

These leaders had loss the whole reason as to why they were called to the priesthood in the first place. They could quote scripture, but cannot live what they quoted. When Jesus shows up at the age of twelve, they had admiration for him, they were so impressed with his knowledge of God's word and wisdom. But, when he returned as a grown man, the same hated him. As a child Jesus posed no threat, but as a grown man, his living example of God's word, exposed the religious leaders misappropriation of that same word, God's people and the alluding to the truth.

The amazing thing is, people who have been anointed by God, sometimes think they can stop the God in you, if misguided by the wrong spirit? This is what happened to King Saul and David. Saul thought he could use his anointing to destroy God's newly anointed. This is not what your anointing is to be used for.

The Pharisees were operating in the same spirit as Saul. They thought they could stop Jesus from doing what he was called to do. How can you use God against God? *"A kingdom divided against itself cannot stand."* Jesus would not allow religion to come in-between his relationship with God. So I want to encourage you to define your vision, know for sure it came from God, and if so, no one can stop you, because they cannot STOP God! Don't give power to anyone to separate you from your God! *"Me and my Father are one and the same."*

Religious Leaders part in leading to Jesus arrest, trial, condemnation and ultimately, his crucifixion.

Take a look at how Jesus rebukes the religious leaders for coming against the will of God, even when they think you are doing the will of God. If we do not humble ourselves, we can be on the wrong side of God while preaching and teaching from the word of God. They were so misguided:

"Then some Pharisees and teachers of the law came to Jesus from Jerusalem and asked,"Why do your disciples break the tradition of the elders? They don't wash their hands before they eat!" Jesus replied, "And why do you break the command of God for the sake of your tradition? For God said, 'Honor your father and mother' and 'Anyone who curses their father or mother is to be put to death.'

But you say that if anyone declares that what might have been used to help their father or mother is 'devoted to God,' they are not to 'honor their father or mother' with it. Thus you nullify the word of God for the sake of your tradition. You hypocrites! Isaiah was right when he prophesied about you:" 'These people honor me with their lips, but their hearts are far from me.

They worship me in vain; their teachings are merely human rules.' " Jesus called the crowd to him and said, "Listen and understand. What goes into someone's mouth does not defile them, but what comes out of their mouth, that is what defiles them." Then the disciples came to him and asked, "Do you know that the Pharisees were offended when they heard this?" He replied, "Every plant that my heavenly Father has not planted will be pulled up by the roots. Leave them; they are blind guides.

If the blind lead the blind, both will fall into a pit." Peter said, "Explain the parable to us." "Are you still so dull?" Jesus asked them. But the things that come out of a person's mouth come from the heart, and these defile them. For out of the heart come evil thoughts—murder, adultery, sexual immorality, theft, false testimony, slander. These are what defile a person; but eating with unwashed hands does not defile them.""
Matthew 15:1-16, 18-20 NIV

"Then the Pharisees went out and laid plans to trap him in his words.

They sent their disciples to him along with the Herodians. "Teacher," they said, "we know that you are a man of integrity and that you teach the way of God in accordance with the truth. You aren't swayed by others, because you pay no attention to who they are. Tell us then, what is your opinion? Is it right to pay the imperial tax to Caesar or not?" But Jesus, knowing their evil intent, said, "You hypocrites, why are you trying to trap me? Show me the coin used for paying the tax." They brought him a denarius, "Caesar's," they replied. Then he said to them, "So give back to Caesar what is Caesar's, and to God what is God's." When they heard this, they were amazed. So they left him and went away."
    Matthew 22:15-19, 21-22 NIV

A Warning Against Hypocrisy

"Then Jesus said to the crowds and to his disciples: "The teachers of the law and the Pharisees sit in Moses' seat. So you must be careful to do everything they tell you. But do not do what they do, for they do not practice what they preach. They tie up heavy, cumbersome loads and put them on other people's shoulders, but they themselves are not willing to lift a finger to move them.

"Everything they do is done for people to see: They make their phylacteries wide and the tassels on their garments long; they love the place of honor at banquets and the most important seats in the synagogues; they love to be greeted with respect in the marketplaces and to be called 'Rabbi' by others. "But you are not to be called 'Rabbi,' for you have one Teacher, and you are all brothers.

And do not call anyone on earth 'father,' for you have one Father, and he is in heaven. Nor are you to be called instructors, for you have one Instructor, the Messiah. The greatest among you will be your servant. For those who exalt themselves will be humbled, and those who humble themselves will be exalted."
    Matthew 23:1-12 NIV

The Hypocrisy of the Sadducees

"That same day the Sadducees, who say there is no resurrection, came to him with a question. "Teacher," they said, "Moses told us that if a man dies without having children, his brother must marry the widow and raise up

offspring for him. Now there were seven brothers among us. The first one married and died, and since he had no children, he left his wife to his brother. The same thing happened to the second and third brother, right on down to the seventh.

Now then, at the resurrection, whose wife will she be of the seven, since all of them were married to her?" Jesus replied, "You are in error because you do not know the Scriptures or the power of God. At the resurrection people will neither marry nor be given in marriage; they will be like the angels in heaven. But about the resurrection of the dead—have you not read what God said to you, 'I am the God of Abraham, the God of Isaac, and the God of Jacob'? He is not the God of the dead but of the living." When the crowds heard this, they were astonished at his teaching."
Matthew 22:23-26, 28-33 NIV

Seven Woes on the Teachers of the Law and the Pharisees

""Woe to you, teachers of the law and Pharisees, you hypocrites! You shut the door of the kingdom of heaven in people's faces. You yourselves do not enter, nor will you let those enter who are trying to. "Woe to you, teachers of the law and Pharisees, you hypocrites! You travel over land and sea to win a single convert, and when you have succeeded, you make them twice as much a child of hell as you are.

"Woe to you, blind guides! You say, 'If anyone swears by the temple, it means nothing; but anyone who swears by the gold of the temple is bound by that oath.' You blind fools! Which is greater: the gold, or the temple that makes the gold sacred? You also say, 'If anyone swears by the altar, it means nothing; but anyone who swears by the gift on the altar is bound by that oath.' You blind men!

Which is greater: the gift, or the altar that makes the gift sacred? Therefore, anyone who swears by the altar swears by it and by everything on it. And anyone who swears by the temple swears by it and by the one who dwells in it. And anyone who swears by heaven swears by God's throne and by the one who sits on it. "Woe to you, teachers of the law and Pharisees, you hypocrites!

You give a tenth of your spices—mint, dill and cumin. But you have neglected the more important matters of the law—justice, mercy and faithfulness. You should have practiced the latter, without neglecting the former. You blind guides! You strain out a gnat but swallow a camel. "Woe to you, teachers of the law and Pharisees, you hypocrites! You clean the outside of the cup and dish, but inside they are full of greed and self-indulgence. Blind Pharisee! First clean the inside of the cup and dish, and then the outside also will be clean. "Woe to you, teachers of the law and Pharisees, you hypocrites!

You are like whitewashed tombs, which look beautiful on the outside but on the inside are full of the bones of the dead and everything unclean. In the same way, on the outside you appear to people as righteous but on the inside you are full of hypocrisy and wickedness. "Woe to you, teachers of the law and Pharisees, you hypocrites! You build tombs for the prophets and decorate the graves of the righteous. And you say, 'If we had lived in the days of our ancestors, we would not have taken part with them in shedding the blood of the prophets.' So you testify against yourselves that you are the descendants of those who murdered the prophets. Go ahead, then, and complete what your ancestors started! "You Snakes! You brood of vipers! How will you escape being condemned to hell?

Therefore I am sending you prophets and sages and teachers. Some of them you will kill and crucify; others you will flog in your synagogues and pursue from town to town. And so upon you will come all the righteous blood that has been shed on earth, from the blood of righteous Abel to the blood of Zechariah son of Berekiah, whom you murdered between the temple and the altar.

Truly I tell you, all this will come on this generation. "Jerusalem, Jerusalem, you who kill the prophets and stone those sent to you, how often I have longed to gather your children together, as a hen gathers her chicks under her wings, and you were not willing. Look, your house is left to you desolate. **For I tell you, you will not see me again until you say, 'Blessed is he who comes in the name of the Lord.'"***
Matthew 23:13, 15-39 NIV

Judas Agrees to Betray Jesus

"Then one of the Twelve—the one called Judas Iscariot—went to the chief priests and asked, "What are you willing to give me if I deliver him over to you?" So they counted out for him thirty pieces of silver. From then on Judas watched for an opportunity to hand him over."

Matthew 26:14-16 NIV

"Offenses must come, but woe unto the person/persons who agreed with the devil to be used to offend you." Great is your reward my brothers and sisters of the kingdom.

I know it hurts right now, but God knows your pain....Thank you Jesus!

One day you will walk up and feel the pain no more. Just watch and see. This too shall pass...

Don't worry when close ones betray you, because Jesus is our example, keep your eyes on the prize.

My God! I feel the Holy Ghost Fire!

"And it came to pass, when Jesus had finished all these sayings, he said unto his disciples, Ye know that after two days is the feast of the passover, and the Son of man is betrayed to be crucified. Then assembled together the chief priests, and the scribes, and the elders of the people, unto the palace of the high priest, who was called Caiaphas, and consulted that they might take Jesus by subtilty, and kill him. But they said, Not on the feast day, lest there be an uproar among the people."
Matthew 26:1-5 KJV

Gethsemane

"Then Jesus went with his disciples to a place called Gethsemane, and he said to them, "Sit here while I go over there and pray." He took Peter and the two sons of Zebedee along with him, and he began to be sorrowful and troubled. Then he said to them, "My soul is overwhelmed with sorrow to the point of death. Stay here and keep watch with me." Going a little farther, he fell with his face to the ground and prayed, "My Father, if it is possible, may this cup be taken from me.

Yet not as I will, but as you will." Then he returned to his disciples and found them sleeping. "Couldn't you men keep watch with me for one hour?" he asked Peter. "Watch and pray so that you will not fall into temptation. The spirit is willing, but the flesh is weak." He went away a second time and prayed, "My Father, if it is not possible for this cup to be taken away unless I drink it, may your will be done." When he came back, he again found them sleeping, because their eyes were heavy.

Then he returned to the disciples and said to them, "Are you still sleeping and resting? Look, the hour has come, and the Son of Man is delivered into the hands of sinners. Rise! Let us go! Here comes my betrayer!""
Matthew 26:36-43, 45-46 NIV

Jesus Arrested

"While he was still speaking, Judas, one of the Twelve, arrived. With him was a large crowd armed with swords and clubs, sent from the chief priests and the elders of the people. Now the betrayer had arranged a signal with them: "The one I kiss is the man; arrest him." Going at once to Jesus, Judas said, "Greetings, Rabbi!" and kissed him. Jesus replied, "Do what you came for, friend."

Then the men stepped forward, seized Jesus and arrested him. With that, one of Jesus' companions reached for his sword, drew it out and struck the servant of the high priest, cutting off his ear. "Put your sword back in its place," Jesus said to him, "for all who draw the sword will die by the sword. But how then would the Scriptures be fulfilled that say it must happen in this way?"

In that hour Jesus said to the crowd, "Am I leading a rebellion, that you have come out with swords and clubs to capture me? Every day I sat in the temple courts teaching, and you did not arrest me. But this has all taken place that the writings of the prophets might be fulfilled." Then all the disciples deserted him and fled." Matthew 26:47-52, 54-56 NIV

Jesus Before the Sanhedrin (Religious Leaders)

"Those who had arrested Jesus took him to Caiaphas the high priest, where the teachers of the law and the elders had assembled. But Peter followed him at a distance, right up to the courtyard of the high priest. He entered and sat down with the guards to see the outcome.

The chief priests and the whole Sanhedrin were looking for false evidence against Jesus so that they could put him to death. But they did not find any, though many false witnesses came forward. Finally two came forward and declared, "This fellow said, 'I am able to destroy the temple of God and rebuild it in three days.' " Then the high priest stood up and said to Jesus, "Are you not going to answer?

What is this testimony that these men are bringing against you?" But Jesus remained silent. The high priest said to him, "I charge you under oath by the living God: Tell us if you are the Messiah, the Son of God." "You have said so," Jesus replied. "But I say to all of you: From now on you will see the Son of Man sitting at the right hand of the Mighty One and coming on the clouds of heaven."

Then the high priest tore his clothes and said, "He has spoken blasphemy! Why do we need any more witnesses? Look, now you have heard the blasphemy. What do you think?" "He is worthy of death," they answered. Then they spit in his face and struck him with their fists. Others slapped him"
"And said, "Prophesy to us, Messiah. Who hit you?""

Peter Disowns Jesus

"Now Peter was sitting out in the courtyard, and a servant girl came to him. "You also were with Jesus of Galilee," she said. But he denied it before them all. "I don't know what you're talking about," he said. Then he went out to the gateway, where another servant girl saw him and said to the people there, "This fellow was with Jesus of Nazareth." He denied it again, with an oath: "I don't know the man!" After a little while, those standing there went up to Peter and said, "Surely you are one of them; your accent gives you away." Then he began to call down curses, and he swore to them, "I don't know the man!" Immediately a rooster crowed. Then Peter remembered the word Jesus had spoken: "Before the rooster crows, you will disown me three times." And he went outside and wept bitterly." Matthew 26:57-75 NIV

Judas Hangs Himself

"Early in the morning, all the chief priests and the elders of the people made their plans how to have Jesus executed. So they bound him, led him away and handed him over to Pilate the governor. When Judas, who had betrayed him, saw that Jesus was condemned, he was seized with remorse and returned the thirty pieces of silver to the chief priests and the elders. "I have

sinned," he said, "for I have betrayed innocent blood."

"What is that to us?" they replied, "That's your responsibility." So Judas threw the money into the temple and left. Then he went away and hanged himself. The chief priests picked up the coins and said, "It is against the law to put this into the treasury, since it is blood money." So they decided to use the money to buy the potter's field as a burial place for foreigners.

Then what was spoken by Jeremiah the prophet was fulfilled: "They took the thirty pieces of silver, the price set on him by the people of Israel, and they used them to buy the potter's field, as the Lord commanded me.""
  Matthew 27:1-7, 9-10 NIV

Jesus Before Pilot

"Then the Jewish leaders took Jesus from Caiaphas to the palace of the Roman governor. By now it was early morning, and to avoid ceremonial uncleanness they did not enter the palace, because they wanted to be able to eat the Passover. So Pilate came out to them and asked, "What charges are you bringing against this man?" "If he were not a criminal," they replied, "we would not have handed him over to you."

Pilate said, "Take him yourselves and judge him by your own law." "But we have no right to execute anyone," they objected. This took place to fulfill what Jesus had said about the kind of death he was going to die. Pilate then went back inside the palace, summoned Jesus and asked him, "Are you the king of the Jews?" "Is that your own idea," Jesus asked, "or did others talk to you about me?" "Am I a Jew?" Pilate replied. "Your own people and chief priests handed you over to me.

What is it you have done?" Jesus said, "My kingdom is not of this world. If it were, my servants would fight to prevent my arrest by the Jewish leaders. But now my kingdom is from another place." "You are a king, then!" said Pilate. Jesus answered, "You say that I am a king. In fact, the reason I was born and came into the world is to testify to the truth. Everyone on the side of truth listens to me." "What is truth?" retorted Pilate.

With this he went out again to the Jews gathered there and said, "I find no basis for a charge against him. But it is your custom for me to release to you one prisoner at the time of the Passover. Do you want me to release 'the

king of the Jews'?" They shouted back, "No, not him! Give us Barabbas!" Now Barabbas had taken part in an uprising."
  John 18:28-40 NIV

"Meanwhile Jesus stood before the governor, and the governor asked him, "Are you the king of the Jews?" "You have said so," Jesus replied. When he was accused by the chief priests and the elders, he gave no answer. Then Pilate asked him, "Don't you hear the testimony they are bringing against you?" But Jesus made no reply, not even to a single charge—to the great amazement of the governor.

Now it was the governor's custom at the festival to release a prisoner chosen by the crowd. At that time they had a well-known prisoner whose name was Jesus Barabbas. So when the crowd had gathered, Pilate asked them, "Which one do you want me to release to you: Jesus Barabbas, or Jesus who is called the Messiah?" For he knew it was out of self-interest that they had handed Jesus over to him. While Pilate was sitting on the judge's seat, his wife sent him this message: "Don't have anything to do with that innocent man, for I have suffered a great deal today in a dream because of him."

But the chief priests and the elders persuaded the crowd to ask for Barabbas and to have Jesus executed. "Which of the two do you want me to release to you?" asked the governor. "Barabbas," they answered. "What shall I do, then, with Jesus who is called the Messiah?" Pilate asked. They all answered, "Crucify him!" "Why? What crime has he committed?" asked Pilate. But they shouted all the louder, "Crucify him!" When Pilate saw that he was getting nowhere, but that instead an uproar was starting, he took water and washed his hands in front of the crowd.

Judas wasn't the only one who betrayed Jesus, he was the closest one to Jesus to betray him. Many of the same people who shouted" Hosanna,"when Jesus entered the city, five days later were shouting "Crucify Him!" People will turn on you when they don't love you. They had no love for the Lord. Jesus was not what they though he should be, and did not give them what they imaged. They didn't want a Savior, they didn't want a prophet, they wanted a king now, not a king later...so , "Crucify Him!"

Some people are following you for what they think you are and what they can get from you. If you disappoint, they will turn on you

and lie on you, seeking to destroy you, simply because you did not finance their fantasy. Don't be surprised at people who turn on you, because you did not give them the life they imagined you would.

Betrayal can hide in people for as long as it takes. Some good people have lost their lives and some even have been imprisoned, simply because someone they loved, didn't love them in the way they gave them love and were disappointed. We may love Jesus, but for Judas and these people…Jesus was a disappointment.

"I am innocent of this man's blood," he said. "It is your responsibility!" All the people answered, "His blood is on us and on our children!" Then he released Barabbas to them, but he had Jesus flogged, and handed him over to be crucified."Matthew 27:11-26 NIV

Jesus Is Mocked

Be encouraged kingdom family, when people mock you for what you believe. Stand on what God word says, one day they will not be mocking anymore. They will wished they had listen and walked the walk you're being mocked for, so many who have presided us in death, are in darkness and hopelessness right now. Trust and believe they are in that holding place right now at this very moment thinking about all the things you said to them, and how they treated you. This is why Jesus tells us to pray for our enemies. We should want anyone to go to that place…

"Then the governor's soldiers took Jesus into the Praetorium and gathered the whole company of soldiers around him. They stripped him and put a scarlet robe on him, and then twisted together a crown of thorns and set it on his head. They put a staff in his right hand. Then they knelt in front of him and mocked him. "Hail, king of the Jews!" they said. They spit on him, and took the staff and struck him on the head again and again. After they had mocked him, they took off the robe and put his own clothes on him. Then they led him away to crucify him."
Matthew 27:27-31 NIV

Jesus sentenced to Be Crucified

"Then Pilate took Jesus and had him flogged. The soldiers twisted

together a crown of thorns and put it on his head. They clothed him in a purple robe and went up to him again and again, saying, "Hail, king of the Jews!" And they slapped him in the face. Once more Pilate came out and said to the Jews gathered there, "Look, I am bringing him out to you to let you know that I find no basis for a charge against him."

When Jesus came out wearing the crown of thorns and the purple robe, Pilate said to them, "Here is the man!" As soon as the chief priests and their officials saw him, they shouted, "Crucify! Crucify!" But Pilate answered, "You take him and crucify him. As for me, I find no basis for a charge against him." The Jewish leaders insisted, "We have a law, and according to that law he must die, because he claimed to be the Son of God." When Pilate heard this, he was even more afraid, "Do you refuse to speak to me?" Pilate said. "Don't you realize I have power either to free you or to crucify you?"

Jesus answered, "You would have no power over me if it were not given to you from above. Therefore the one who handed me over to you is guilty of a greater sin." From then on, Pilate tried to set Jesus free, but the Jewish leaders kept shouting, "If you let this man go, you are no friend of Caesar. Anyone who claims to be a king opposes Caesar." When Pilate heard this, he brought Jesus out and sat down on the judge's seat at a place known as the Stone Pavement (which in Aramaic is Gabbatha).

It was the day of Preparation of the Passover; it was about noon. "Here is your king," Pilate said to the Jews. But they shouted, "Take him away! Take him away! Crucify him!" "Shall I crucify your king?" Pilate asked. "We have no king but Caesar," the chief priests answered. Finally Pilate handed him over to them to be crucified. So the soldiers took charge of Jesus."John 19:1-8, 10-16 NIV

The Crucifixion of Jesus

"Carrying his own cross, he went out to the place of the Skull (which in Aramaic is called Golgotha). There they crucified him, and with him two others—one on each side and Jesus in the middle. Pilate had a notice prepared and fastened to the cross. It read: Jesus of Nazareth, the king of the jews. Many of the Jews read this sign, for the place where Jesus was crucified was near the city, and the sign was written in Aramaic, Latin and Greek.

The chief priests of the Jews protested to Pilate, "Do not write, 'The

King of the Jews,' but that this man claimed to be king of the Jews." Pilate answered, "What I have written, I have written." When the soldiers crucified Jesus, they took his clothes, dividing them into four shares, one for each of them, with the undergarment remaining. This garment was seamless, woven in one piece from top to bottom. "Let's not tear it," they said to one another. "Let's decide by lot who will get it."

This happened that the scripture might be fulfilled that said, "They divided my clothes among them and cast lots for my garment." So this is what the soldiers did. Near the cross of Jesus stood his mother, his mother's sister, Mary the wife of Clopas, and Mary Magdalene. When Jesus saw his mother there, and the disciple whom he loved standing nearby, he said to her, "Woman, here is your son," and to the disciple, "Here is your mother." From that time on, this disciple took her into his home." John 19:17-27 NIV

"As they were going out, they met a man from Cyrene, named Simon, and they forced him to carry the cross. They came to a place called Golgotha (which means "the place of the skull"). There they offered Jesus wine to drink, mixed with gall; but after tasting it, he refused to drink it.

When they had crucified him, they divided up his clothes by casting lots. And sitting down, they kept watch over him there. Above his head they placed the written charge against him: this is Jesus, the king of the jews. Two rebels were crucified with him, one on his right and one on his left. Those who passed by hurled insults at him, shaking their heads In the same way the chief priests, the teachers of the law and the elders mocked him. "He saved others," they said, "But he can't save himself!

He's the king of Israel! Let him come down now from the cross, and we will believe in him. He trusts in God. Let God rescue him now if he wants him, for he said, 'I am the Son of God.' " In the same way the rebels who were crucified with him also heaped insults on him." Matthew 27:32-39, 41-44 NIV

The Death of Jesus

From noon until three in the afternoon darkness came over all the land. About three in the afternoon Jesus cried out in a loud voice, "Eli, Eli, lema sabachthani?" (which means "My God, my God, why have you forsaken me?"). When some of those standing there, heard this, they said, "He's calling

Elijah."

Immediately one of them ran and got a sponge. He filled it with wine vinegar, put it on a staff, and offered it to Jesus to drink. The rest said, "Now leave him alone. Let's see if Elijah comes to save him." And when Jesus had cried out again in a loud voice, he gave up his spirit. At that moment the curtain of the temple was torn in two from top to bottom. The earth shook, the rocks split and the tombs broke open. The bodies of many holy people who had died were raised to life.

They came out of the tombs after Jesus' resurrection and went into the holy city and appeared to many   people. When the centurion and those with him who were guarding Jesus saw the earthquake and all that had happened, they were terrified, and exclaimed, "Surely he was the Son of God!"

Many women were there, watching from a distance. They had followed Jesus from Galilee to care for his needs. Among them were Mary Magdalene, Mary the mother of James and Joseph, and the mother of Zebedee's sons." Matthew 27:45-56 NIV

"Later, knowing that everything had now been finished, and so that Scripture would be fulfilled, Jesus said, "I am thirsty." A jar of wine vinegar was there, so they soaked a sponge in it, put the sponge on a stalk of the hyssop plant, and lifted it to Jesus' lips. When he had received the drink, Jesus said, "It is finished."

With that, he bowed his head and gave up his spirit. Now it was the day of Preparation, and the next day was to be a special Sabbath. Because the Jewish leaders did not want the bodies left on the crosses during the Sabbath, they asked Pilate to have the legs broken and the bodies taken down.

The soldiers therefore came and broke the legs of the first man who had been crucified with Jesus, and then those of the other. But when they came to Jesus and found that he was already dead, they did not break his legs. Instead, one of the soldiers pierced Jesus' side with a spear, bringing a sudden flow of blood and water.

The man who saw it has given testimony, and his testimony is true. He knows that he tells the truth, and he testifies so that you also may believe, and, as another scripture says, "They will look on the one they have pierced." John

19:28-35, 37 NIV

"And blessed is he, whosoever shall not, be offended with me."
Mathew 11:6

It was the Cross at Calvary that gives us access....Now access has been granted...hallelujah!

CHAPTER FIVE

The Resurrection

When you hear the word **Resurrection,** what is your first thought?

When we think God is too late…

Lazarus was sick…very sick. His sisters Martha and Mary was praying for their brother continually for a miracle. This was the same Mary who wept at Jesus feet and dry his feet with her hair. Jesus loved them so and they loved Him at this time she was so hurt because Jesus did not get there in the time she thought he should have. She was disappointed in the fact that her brother died and not only did Jesus not come to pray for him, but, he didn't even make the funeral.

After he had said this, he went on to tell them, "Our friend Lazarus has fallen asleep; but I am going there to wake him up." His disciples replied, "Lord, if he sleeps, he will get better." So then he told them plainly, "Lazarus is dead, Then Thomas (also known as Didymus) said to the rest of the disciples, "Let us also go, that we may die with him."

On his arrival, Jesus found that Lazarus had already been in the tomb for four days. and many Jews had come to Martha and Mary to comfort them in the loss of their brother. When Martha heard that Jesus was coming, she went out to meet him, but Mary stayed at home. "Lord," Martha said to Jesus, "if you had been here, my brother would not have died. Jesus said to her, "Your brother will rise again." Martha answered, "I know he will rise again in the **resurrection** *at the last day."*

* * *

*Jesus said to her, **"I am the resurrection and the life.** The one who believes in me will live, even though they die; "Yes, Lord," she replied, "I believe that you are the Messiah, the Son of God, who is to come into the world." After she had said this, she went back and called her sister Mary aside. "The Teacher is here," she said, "and is asking for you." Now Jesus had not yet entered the village, but was still at the place where Martha had met him.*

When the Jews who had been with Mary in the house, comforting her, noticed how quickly she got up and went out, they followed her, supposing she was going to the tomb to mourn there. When Mary reached the place where Jesus was and saw him, she fell at his feet and said, "Lord, if you had been here, my brother would not have died." When Jesus saw her weeping, and the Jews who had come along with her also weeping, he was deeply moved in spirit and troubled.

"Where have you laid him?" he asked. "Come and see, Lord," they replied. Jesus wept. Then the Jews said, "See how he loved him!" But some of them said, "Could not he who opened the eyes of the blind man have kept this man from dying?"" John 11:11-12, 14, 16-17, 19-21, 23-25, 27-28, 30-37

We have been taught or conditioned to think resurrection is an event, something we are waiting for, that only can happen on a scheduled date. She repeatedly was saying, "On that day" and believing Jesus could heal him but thinking he's more than even that, he's the Resurrection and life! How powerful for him to be there? Even to read how Jesus wept, shows he's in tune and in touch with his people. I refuse to believe Jesus was weeping because of Lazarus death, because he called it, "Sleeping" but I believe he was touched by their mourning and pain, weeping as those who had no hope.

But the greater part of Jesus weeping was because there were two great and influential groups of priesthood present, the Pharisees and Sadducees. Their was divisions among the two groups of leaders. The Pharisees believed in the resurrection, but the Sadducees said, "There's no such thing as resurrection" Here they were at Lazarus's funeral. They were looking for Jesus to see how to arrest him, they were desperately trying to catch him doing wrong, or breaking the Law of Moses. They said, "He loves Lazarus, could it be that he comes to heal him, because he loves him?

* * *

"*Jesus, once more deeply moved, came to the tomb. It was a cave with a stone laid across the entrance. "Take away the stone," he said. "But, Lord," said Martha, the sister of the dead man, "by this time there is a bad odor, for he has been there four days." Then Jesus said, "Did I not tell you that if you believe, you will see the glory of God?" So they took away the stone.*

Then Jesus looked up and said, "Father, I thank you that you have heard me. When he had said this, Jesus called in a loud voice, "Lazarus, come out!" The dead man came out, his hands and feet wrapped with strips of linen, and a cloth around his face. Jesus said to them, "Take off the grave clothes and let him go."" John 11:38-41, 43-44

"*Therefore many of the Jews who had come to visit Mary, and had seen what Jesus did, believed in him. But some of them went to the Pharisees and told them what Jesus had done. Then the chief priests and the Pharisees called a meeting of the Sanhedrin. "What are we accomplishing?" they asked. "Here is this man performing many signs. If we let him go on like this, everyone will believe in him, and then the Romans will come and take away both our temple and our nation."*

Then one of them, named Caiaphas, who was high priest that year, spoke up, "You know nothing at all! You do not realize that it is better for you that one man die for the people than that the whole nation perish." He did not say this on his own, but as high priest that year he prophesied that Jesus would die for the Jewish nation, and not only for that nation but also for the scattered children of God, to bring them together and make them one.

Therefore Jesus no longer moved about publicly among the people of Judea. Instead he withdrew to a region near the wilderness, to a village called Ephraim, where he stayed with his disciples. When it was almost time for the Jewish Passover, many went up from the country to Jerusalem for their ceremonial cleansing before the Passover.

They kept looking for Jesus, and as they stood in the temple courts they asked one another, "What do you think? Isn't he coming to the festival at all?" But the chief priests and the Pharisees had given orders that anyone who found out where Jesus was should report it so that they might arrest him." (John 11:45-52, 54-57)

"*For as in Adam all die, so in Christ all will be made alive.*"

1 Corinthians 15:22 NIV

"He is not here; he has risen, just as he said. Come and see the place where he lay."
   Matthew 28:6 NIV

"But Christ has indeed been raised from the dead, the first fruits of those who have fallen asleep."
   1 Corinthians 15:20 NIV

For since death came through a man, the resurrection of the dead comes also through a man."
   1 Corinthians 15:21 NIV

"Jesus said to her, "I am the resurrection and the life. The one who believes in me will live, even though they die;"
   John 11:25 NIV

"For we believe that Jesus died and rose again, and so we believe that God will bring with Jesus those who have fallen asleep in him."
   1 Thessalonians 4:14 NIV

"For my Father's will is that everyone who looks to the Son and believes in him shall have eternal life, and I will raise them up at the last day.""
   John 6:40 NIV

"By his power God raised the Lord from the dead, and he will raise us also."
   1 Corinthians 6:14 NIV

"Praise be to the God and Father of our Lord Jesus Christ! In his great mercy he has given us new birth into a living hope through the resurrection of Jesus Christ from the dead,""and into an inheritance that can never perish, spoil or fade.

This inheritance is kept in heaven for you, who through faith are shielded by God's power until the coming of the salvation that is ready to be revealed in the last time. In all this you greatly rejoice, though now for a little while you may have had to suffer grief in all kinds of trials. These have come so that the proven genuineness of your faith—of greater worth than gold, which perishes even though refined by fire—may result in praise, glory and honor when Jesus Christ is revealed.

Though you have not seen him, you love him; and even though you do not see him now, you believe in him   and are filled with an inexpressible and glorious joy, for you are receiving the end result of your faith, the salvation of your souls."
1 Peter 1:4-9 NIV

For if we have been united with him in a death like his, we will certainly also be united with him in a resurrection like his."
Romans 6:5 NIV

The Burial of Jesus

"Later, Joseph of Arimathea, sked Pilate for the body of Jesus. Now Joseph was a disciple of Jesus, but secretly because he feared the Jewish leaders. With Pilate's permission, he came and took the body away. He was accompanied by Nicodemus, the man who earlier had visited Jesus at night.

Nicodemus brought a mixture of myrrh and aloes, about seventy-five pounds. Taking Jesus' body, the two of them wrapped it, with the spices, in strips of linen. This was in accordance with Jewish burial customs. At the place where Jesus was crucified, there was a garden, and in the garden a new tomb, in which no one had ever been laid. Because it was the Jewish day of Preparation and since the tomb was nearby, they laid Jesus there."John 19:38-42 NIV

And placed it in his own new tomb that he had cut out of the rock. He rolled a big stone in front of the entrance to the tomb and went away. Mary Magdalene and the other Mary were sitting there opposite the tomb."Matthew 27:60-61 NIV

Guarding the Tomb

"The next day, the one after Preparation Day, the chief priests and the Pharisees went to Pilate. "Sir," they said, "we remember that while he was still alive that deceiver said, 'After three days I will rise again.' So give the order for the tomb to be made secure until the third day.

Otherwise, his disciples may come and steal the body and tell the people that *he has been raised from the dead. This last deception will be worse than the first." "Take a guard," Pilate answered. "Go, make the tomb as secure as you know how.""*

   Matthew 27:62-65 NIV

The Empty Tomb

Early on the first day of the week, while it was still dark, Mary Magdalene went to the tomb and saw that the stone had been removed from the entrance. So she came running to Simon Peter and the other disciple, the one Jesus loved, and said, "They have taken the Lord out of the tomb, and we don't know where they have put him!" So Peter and the other disciple started for the tomb.

So Peter and the other disciple started for the tomb. Both were running, but the other disciple outran Peter and reached the tomb first. He bent over and looked in at the strips of linen lying there but did not go in. Then Simon Peter came along behind him and went straight into the tomb. He saw the strips of linen lying there, as well as the cloth that had been wrapped around Jesus' head. The cloth was still lying in its place, separate from the linen.

Finally the other disciple, who had reached the tomb first, also went inside. He saw and believed. (They still did not understand from Scripture that Jesus had to rise from the dead.) Then the disciples went back to where they were staying. Now Mary stood outside the tomb crying. As she wept, she bent over to look into the tomb and saw two angels in white, seated where Jesus' body had been, one at the head and the other at the foot.

They asked her, "Woman, why are you crying?" "They have taken my Lord away," she said, "and I don't know where they have put him." At this, she turned around and saw Jesus standing there, but she did not realize that it was Jesus. He asked her, "Woman, why are you crying? Who is it you are looking for?" Thinking he was the gardener, she said, "Sir, if you have carried him away, tell me where you have put him, and I will get him." Jesus said to her, "Mary." She turned toward him and cried out in Aramaic, "Rabboni!" (which means "Teacher").

Jesus said, "Do not hold on to me, for I have not yet ascended to the Father. Go instead to my brothers and tell them, 'I am ascending to my Father and your Father, to my God and your God.' " Mary Magdalene went to the

disciples with the news: "I have seen the Lord!" And she told them that he had said these things to her."
   John 20:1-18 NIV

Jesus Has Risen

"After the Sabbath, at dawn on the first day of the week, Mary Magdalene and the other Mary went to look at the tomb. There was a violent earthquake, for an angel of the Lord came down from heaven and, going to the tomb, rolled back the stone and sat on it.

His appearance was like lightning, and his clothes were white as snow. The guards were so afraid of him that they shook and became like dead men. The angel said to the women, "Do not be afraid, for I know that you are looking for Jesus, who was crucified. He is not here; he has risen, just as he said. Come and see the place where he lay."
   Matthew 28:1-6 NIV

The Resurrection

"The first day of the week cometh Mary Magdalene early, when it was yet dark, unto the Sepulchre, and sees the stone taken away from the Sepulchre. Then she runneth, and cometh to Simon Peter, and to the other disciple, whom Jesus loved, and saith unto them,

They have taken away the Lord out of the Sepulchre, and we know not where they have laid him. Peter therefore went forth, and that other disciple, and came to the Sepulchre. So they ran both together: and the other disciple did outrun Peter, and came first to the Sepulchre. And he stooping down, and looking in, saw the linen clothes lying; yet went he not in.

Then cometh Simon Peter following him, and went into the Sepulchre, and sees the linen clothes lie, and the napkin, that was about his head, not lying with the linen clothes, but wrapped together in a place by itself. Then went in also that other disciple, which came first to the Sepulchre, and he saw, and believed. For as yet they knew not the scripture, that he must rise again from the dead. Then the disciples went away again unto their own home.

But Mary stood without at the Sepulchre weeping: and as she wept, she stooped down, and looked into the Sepulchre, and sees two angels in white sitting, the one at the head, and the other at the feet, where the body of Jesus had lain. And they say unto her, Woman, why weepest thou? She saith unto them, Because they have taken away my Lord, and I know not where they have laid him. And when she had thus said, she turned herself back, and saw Jesus standing, and knew not that it was Jesus.

Jesus saith unto her, Woman, why weepest thou? Whom seekest thou? She, supposing him to be the gardener, saith unto him, Sir, if thou have borne him hence, tell me where thou hast laid him, and I will take him away. Jesus saith unto her, Mary, she turned herself, and saith unto him, Rabboni; which is to say, Master. **Jesus saith unto her, Touch me not; for I am not yet ascended to my Father: but go to my brethren, and say unto them, I ascend unto my Father, and your Father; and to my God, and your God.**

Mary Magdalene came and told the disciples that she had seen the Lord, and that he had spoken these things unto her. Then the same day at evening, being the first day of the week, when the doors were shut where the disciples were assembled for fear of the Jews, came Jesus and stood in the midst, and saith unto them, Peace be unto you. And when he had so said, he shewed unto them his hands and his side.

Then were the disciples glad, when they saw the Lord. Then said Jesus to them again, Peace be unto you: as my Father hath sent me, even so send I you. And when he had said this, he breathed on them, and saith unto them, Receive ye the Holy Ghost: whose soever sins ye remit, they are remitted unto them; and whose soever sins ye retain, they are retained. But Thomas, one of the twelve, called Didymus, was not with them when Jesus came. The other disciples therefore said unto him, We have seen the Lord. But he said unto them, Except I shall see in his hands the print of the nails, and put my finger into the print of the nails, and thrust my hand into his side, I will not believe.

And after eight days again his disciples were within, and Thomas with them: then came Jesus, the doors being shut, and stood in the midst, and said, Peace be unto you. Then saith he to Thomas, Reach hither thy finger, and behold my hands; and reach hither thy hand, and thrust it into my side: and be not faithless, but believing.

And Thomas answered and said unto him, My Lord and my God. Jesus saith unto him, Thomas, because thou hast seen me, thou hast believed: blessed are they that have not seen, and yet have believed. And many other signs truly did Jesus in the presence of his disciples, which are not written in this book: but these are written, that ye might believe that Jesus is the Christ, the Son of God; and that believing ye might have life through his name."John 20:1-31 KJV

Jesus is the first to ever turn the grave (Tomb) into a dressing room. When Jesus died or gave up the ghost, he said, "Father, into your hands I commit my spirit" and he gave up the ghost. His soul went into Hades (Hell/Paradise) , his body was laid in the tomb.

Look at our God, he is resurrected but takes the time to remove the stone that was to close the mouth of the tomb. He didn't move to get, but move it so that the women who come looking for him, could get in. Then before he exits, he takes the time to leave us, the church a message by his graves clothes left behind. He also takes the time to fold the napkin that was wrapped around his head, but leave the linen wreaked around his body, unmade and unravelled, like an unmade bed. He was letting the disciples (man and female) know, you must get the church in order, because me and my Father are ONE , unified (the head) , but the body (church) has to come into the unity of the Holy Spirit., to be one.

Jesus knew that Satan would attack the Body of Christ with DIVISION, mainly…Denominations! Stupid reasons for the "Body of Christ" to be divided, over baptism of water and/or spirit, of John or Jesus, of Paul or Peter, Baptist or Pentecostal, having the Holy Ghost or Not, necessary or not, women can preach, or ought not preach, fasting or not fasting, speaking in tongues or no speaking in tongues, jew or gentile church, should women be silent or should they speak…you get the idea?

We are divided on so many foolish things. Without Christ there would be no "Body of Christ (The Church).

Look at what Jesus prayed well in advance , before he was crucified, "My prayer is not for them alone. I pray also for those who will believe in me through their message, that all of them may be one, Father, just as you are in me and I am in you. May they also be in us so that the world may believe that you have sent me. I have given them the glory that you gave me, that they may be one as we are one— I in them and you in me—so that they may be brought to complete unity. Then the

world will know that you sent me and have loved them even as you have loved me."
    John 17:20-23 NIV

We are a spirit, we have a soul and lives in a body. The triune man, three parts in one, like the triune God. We are made in the image of God, The Father, The Son and The Holy Spirit.

Jesus is Alive!

"They were talking with each other about everything that had happened. As they talked and discussed these things with each other, Jesus himself came up and walked along with them; but they were kept from recognizing him. He asked them, "What are you discussing together as you walk along?" They stood still, their faces downcast. One of them, named Cleopas, asked him, "Are you the only one visiting Jerusalem who does not know the things that have happened there in these days?" "What things?" He asked. "About Jesus of Nazareth," they replied. "He was a prophet, powerful in word and deed before God and all the people. The chief priests and our rulers handed him over to be sentenced to death, and they crucified him; but we had hoped that he was the one who was going to redeem Israel.

And what is more, it is the third day since all this took place. In addition, some of our women amazed us. They went to the tomb early this morning but didn't find his body. They came and told us that they had seen a vision of angels, who said he was alive. Then some of our companions went to the tomb and found it just as the women had said, but they did not see Jesus." He said to them, "How foolish you are, and how slow to believe all that the prophets have spoken! Did not the Messiah have to suffer these things and then enter his glory?"

And beginning with Moses and all the Prophets, he explained to them what was said in all the Scriptures concerning himself. As they approached the village to which they were going, Jesus continued on as if he were going farther. But they urged him strongly, "Stay with us, for it is nearly evening; the day is almost over." So he went in to stay with them. When he was at the table with them, he took bread, gave thanks, broke it and began to give it to them. Then their eyes were opened and they recognized him, and he disappeared from their sight.

* * *

They asked each other, "Were not our hearts burning within us while he talked with us on the road and opened the Scriptures to us?" They got up and returned at once to Jerusalem. There they found the Eleven and those with them, assembled together and saying, "It is true! The Lord has risen and has appeared to Simon." Then the two told what had happened on the way, and how Jesus was recognized by them when he broke the bread."Luke 24:14-35 NIV

After everything Jesus went through for you and I, we can never take him for granted…at least, we ought not to. When we see how Jesus was abuse, betrayed, mocked, hated and killed, don't ever think because of your struggles and being hated, cause you to think less of yourselves. Pick your head up in humility and honor. Know this, you will never die believing in The Lord Jesus Christ.

Do not be afraid, home is beautiful and you have true family there cheering you on here. We were never meant to be here without this fight. God can't trust us until we have tried in time. Eternity is where you want to be, you just may not know it yet. True the Lord with all of your heart. Be relentless, steadfast and unmovable.

We are living intruding times, but know just that, they are times, meaning they will not last forever. Your real life is a continuation of your dreams and ambitions. Do business, and God's business while you're here, but by no means get caught up in this world, Satan will swallow you up and the laugh at you in the process! He's been doing this for a long time. Don't be one to share in his JUDGMENT! Choose today who you are going to serve. God or Money, Good or evil, right or wrong, weak or wicked, life or death?

I know people who have chosen this world and material things over God. They do religion while sold out for this world. What is amazing, is, they are no where near being rich, but have sold their soul like Judas for a quick high or good feeling, that they cannot keep? I call it, **"Dying for Memories."**

What could we say on Judgment Day? That we didn't know, or we didn't think it was this serious? …And He says, "Call on the god that you served in your lifetime."

When Jesus defeated Death, hell and the grave, he collected the keys that would free you and me.

Have you noticed, God never proves Himself to the wicked, only to His children, those who believes in Him?

No one can come remotely close to what God has done for us. So, I choose JESUS!

"But if the Spirit of him that raised up Jesus from the dead dwell in you, he that raised up Christ from the dead shall also quicken your mortal bodies by his Spirit that dwells in you."
   Romans 8:11 KJV

There is so much proof of who Jesus was to their generation and to every generation from the past ,present and future. Death is not the End for a believer, but the opposite, it's a continuation of live, your best life yet, that you've never could accurately imagine.

But as it is written, Eye hath not seen, nor ear heard, Neither have entered into the heart of man, The things which God hath prepared for them that love him."
   1 Corinthians 2:9 KJV

When people make mockery of you as a believer and says, "Isn't Jesus supposed to be coming back, when is he coming? You Christians have been saying this forever and He still haven't come back…I'm waiting to see him too…just keep waiting for him…hahaha.

They have no clue. Every time a person or persons take their last breath, oh they get to see him! This the whole purpose of the book. Take away the foolishness of death is over, no, death is just the beginning of dealing the One who created you! Whether you believe or not, it carries no wait. You don't have to believe in death, but keep on living until you expire, and then what? This is what Jesus had to say to a few who thought they knew more than God.

Check this out!
   "And he saith unto me, Seal not the sayings of the prophecy of this book: for the time is at hand. He that is unjust, let him be unjust

still: and he which is filthy, let him be filthy still: and he that is righteous, let him be righteous still: and he that is holy, let him be holy still. And, behold, I come quickly; and my reward is with me, to give every man according as his work shall be.

I am Alpha and Omega, the beginning and the end, the first and the last. Blessed are they that do his commandments, that they may have right to the tree of life, and may enter in through the gates into the city. For without are dogs, and sorcerers, and whoremongers, and murderers, and idolaters, and whosoever loves and makes a lie."
Revelation 22:10-15 KJV
As soon as you take your last breath...

If I never have the pleasure of meeting you here in this life and world, let's be united with love and faith in our Lord Jesus Christ and continue to preach the gospel of the kingdom. Love one another, strive to make this world a better place for our children and save as many people as you can, I know it gets hard sometimes, but hey!
"We can do all things..through Christ who strengthens us"...Right!

These things were left on record that we might believe.

Know your
Kingdom Rights!

I'll see you on the other side of this...SELAH

Jesus Is The Resurrection!

CHAPTER SIX

Easter Morning

It's Wednesday before Easter Sunday and I'm waiting on a package…
it's late. Finally I receive it and it's all there and It's good. I have my
people and they are very anxious, to get their hands on this product.
Well, I wanted to believe that I was just anxious for the money it would
bring me, but, this was not true. I was hooked! I was a drug (cocaine)
addict in denial. I had a secret! I had tried many times on my own to
stop doing the dope thing but was unsuccessful.

Unknowingly, this would become the downward spiral, scariest and
worse time of my life! I was always a happy, upbeat person. Lover of
life and music, music was my companion since the age of 11. It was
Wednesday and I was feeling good about the rest of the week, so I
thought. I was going to work as scheduled, but something appears to
be off. To get the jest of what happened, let me take you little ways
back to November before Easter.

I was with my crew and was weighing, cutting and packaging
preparing for sales. We are about to hit the streets with one the best
products out there. While I'm standing at the table looking at all this
patiently money to be made. Out of no where, I feel a presence like a
warm blanket as though it was liquid coming down over me from the
top of my head. As this is happening to me, it is as though someone
was controlling the sound around me. All of the noise, music and
voices are becoming muffled and almost silent. Then I heard a voice

speak to me in a calm I've never experienced or heard of before.

The voice said to me, " I have anointed you and called you." Then I replied, " Well, why am I here in this place, doing these things?" Then He replied, " I AM, going to deliver you and take you out of this, you will be a witness." Immediately I began to cry and I had no control. First I was looking around to see if anyone was seeing what was happening to me, or better yet, can they hear me and this voice. Does anybody know? I'm starting to feel embarrassed because here I am portraying the life of a drug dealer and I'm over here crying like a baby. What?

Amazingly, no-one seemed to have noticed me or even attempted to talk to me during this encounter. This was another odd occurrence , because someone was always saying or wanting something from me. I gave out packages to hit the streets. By Thursday night, I started getting high, by smoking and sniffing cocaine. I was drinking hard liquor with a vengeance. I was wondering what was wrong with me. I couldn't stop! This drug thing is like a Secret Society. So many people do drugs, it's unbelievable. I think that's what drew me in, I thought drugs were for low lives, then I saw professional people doing it. Upper class people…wow! I had a secret. I was doing drugs and not many people knew about it, except those who do it as well.

It's November and we have about two weeks before Thanksgiving. Holidays were always big with my family, but I was feeling a little awkward because drugs were becoming my greatest concern. I love family, but man this dope is calling me and I'm shocked it has so much power over my life. It's as though I'm walking around with a personal drug dealing, drug using advisor in my head.

This go round, everybody seems to be struggling moving product. I personally was having some strange things happening. I couldn't help but to think about the thing that happened to me in the basement at the table. Could this be God messing with me. I can't explain it, but I was starting to feel some kind of way about this. It was approaching Re-Up time and I didn't see as much profit as the other times. I realized that at down time, I had become the biggest customer of my own product. No matter how much you hear ,Never get high on your own supply,"for whatever reason, you never think it will be you.

* * *

I began to lie to myself more frequently. "This time I won't use much, I going to get this money this time!" We're approaching Thanksgiving week and now my excuse is, we need to enjoy the Holidays. After Thanksgiving Holidays, I started to realize how much money I am losing. I bought my first package with my construction company's money. In the beginning it seemed brilliant. I   was really making money. From the beginning I would always separate the money. I could see how much profit I was getting from the drugs.

I set a goal for myself that when December come-in, I will not get high again. I told myself, "You can do it" and it got worst. Secretly, I was getting scared. I thought of myself as a sober minded, talented and gifted person. I considered myself to be a pretty descent guy. I'm starting to feel like I'm losing control of my life. Now, I'm really getting concern, I haven't been able to stop this drug habit. I was always sober minded, never smoke, or drank and definitely didn't do drugs, but here I am. I'm starting to panic because I didn't know until now how addicted I really was. I started thinking of the possibilities of me needing professional help. This made me really think about my options, and I concluded, I am going to stop this foolishness.

We're approaching the Christmas season, and oh my how I love Christmas. I loved everything about it. The lights, the music, the spirit of Christmas just made me happy, it's the best time of the year. I took care of Christmas shopping early and now was feeling I could reward myself or treat myself. Big, big mistake. I started getting high and just kept going.

 My family, colleagues and many friends had no clue that I was a working addict. I didn't miss work, I was on time, I met my appointments and appeared to be successful at my profession. I had my own business and thought I was smarter than most, because my plan was to invest in the dope game and flip my money into a profit. Well, that was the plan. It started out with me making three times what I had initially invested.

I thought I was doing something new, not knowing how the enemy has mastered deception. For a moment, I was the MAN, at least that's what they were saying. I felt like I was on top of the world. Not knowing my world was about to come down crashing. Going back to November of the previous year, I had a supernatural encounter.

At this point, I have been doing cocaine and drinking alcohol for three days and night straight with no sleep. I had no appetite for food. I am so, so tired. I'm home now I have a friend visiting from France, and she doesn't know that I do drugs. I met her when I was an active musician and she's only known my as the clean cut kinda guy. So, I'm reluctant to expose my drug indulging.

She's never even know me to drink alcohol. I can do away with the drinking, that wasn't my main thing, it was the sniffing and smoking of that cocaine, it made me want to drink. We, we are hanging out and I find myself struggling to be me. The me I used to be. This was messing with my ego and pride, because I know how I was raised. I grew up in a drug free home.

I grew up in church...I'm talking about Pentecostal church! Where there is no drinking, no smoking, no cussing and swearing, women didn't were pants, they were forbidden to wear jewelry for the exception of an engagement and/or wedding ring. Oh...we were allowed to wear a watch, but no bracelets or necklaces...oh, I almost forgot, definitely no earrings.

My point is, I was the clean due, "Church Boy" as they would call me, as if that was my real name. I didn't drink or do drugs in school or when I was in bands traveling. I lived the club life for years, and wouldn't touch a thing. I used to order orange juice or gingerly from the bar...all the time. Bartenders knew me for that!
So here I am with this beautiful person who knows me from music, not church. She was clean cut..."clean as a whistle" as they would say. This was one of the things that drew us together, as a staple of our newly found our relationship at that time. I had a lot of respect for her and now, I'm struggling with trying to be who I'd used to be to her.

Well, it was working for a little while. When we were out to eat, (well I wasn't really eating) I was thinking about my other date...Cocaine! For a brief time, I was really liking who she was reminding me of the guy who had gotten lost. I don't know if she knew? But, I can't take it anymore. So I excused myself from the table to go to the restroom.

It's there where I had to get my (girl) as they used to call it. I went into the stall and I'm telling you…I was sniffing that cocaine, like there was no tomorrow! I returned to the table and of course, I didn't want to touch my food. I was full of energy…to the max, because I was always energized naturally, but no wit's turn up! I rushed her to get out of there and go home with me. This is where it became difficult to hide my addition.

This was the begging of my three day binge. I was with her, but not with her, because I was constantly excusing myself to go my own bathroom. Finally, she asked me, "What are you doing?..this is not like you?" I paused for a second..and then said, "Look I do a little cocaine, it's no big deal. She responded, "Wait a minute Joseph, you get high now?"I was offended, can you believe that….I was offended?

Once I got over what I thought she might have felt about me getting, he "was on and poppin" as they say. This would be the beginning of a three days and nights getting high binge.I was getting high and drinking and sexing. How high can one get. It seems as though she accepted it, she did not condemn me, she acted as if this was ok… normal. She didn't mention my getting high again. What was sad and so wrong, was by day number two, I pushed the cocaine on her."Don't let me do this by myself..come on…do it with me. I put it on my body and asked her to just sniff it.

To all those who do drugs and have done drugs, you know it's the same story. The devil has no new tricks, he just try them on new people. I was so high, my heart was hurting. I was high and she was high. She didn't't try smoking it, so I was the only one smoking. I was hitting that pipe over and over again. I wanted to rest. I wanted to stop! But I couldn't! There's a voice inside of me that was bigger than me. It keep saying, "One more hit..you can do it."

At this point I'm crying and hitting that glass pipe. All I can see is a smoke fill bowl and thinking, how am I going to smoke all of that. I had plenty of it already rocked up and ready to go. I had powder and rock. I was starting to feel sick. The room was spinning and my chest felt like a drum. I could hear it and feel it. I was scared and this voice was constantly telling me to do more. I can't do more.

I tell my friend that I need to sleep. I'm forcing myself to put down the pipe. I started to walk around in the bedroom, but to no avail, I'm feeling very anxious and strange. I'm thinking I might be having a Heart Attack, and don't even know what that is? I attempted to calm myself down and get my friend scared. It feel like most of this is going on the inside of me. Why Am I hearing these voices telling me it's ok, just do some more? "But I don't want to do more!" Who Am I talking to? All of this battle is really going on inside of me. My friend does not have a clue.

"I just need some sleep," I said to my friend. "Okay" she said. I laid down on the bed and closed my eyes. It felt like everything was moving and moving fast. I just wanted it to stop! As I laid there my friend was continuing to touch me, and I asked her to stop. "I really need to sleep" I said. She said, "Okay." I was determined not to pick up that pipe. It appears to me as though these voices are taking turns, to convince me to do more, like it was their job or something. This was the worst day of my life. I was miserable! What started out pros years a fun and a good time, now was my misery. I began to ask God for help within myself, for some odd reason I was afraid to say it aloud. I was kinda ashamed and condemned, I had not attended church in over ten years.

As I laid there , I felt like I was calming down a little. I couldn't help but think, can God hear my thoughts? I wonder? I kept my eyes closed, as though it helped me not to see the drugs and the pipe. Maybe everything will be alright after all? I was starting to feel some kind of peace...just a little bit. I had been getting high all night again and dawn is about to break. I'm feeling crazy, but somehow I need it to be daytime. As I was lying there, I heard a different kind of voice speaking in my ear, this voice was softly, but with authority."Get Up! Today is the day of salvation," it said. First thing, I opened my eyes to see who was there, because not only did I clearly hear this voice, but I could feel the breath of the mouth it came from. I jumped up and ran to my bathroom, turned on the water at the sink, and then began to throw cold water on my face, repeatedly.

Then without drying my face, I looked into the mirror. It appeared that I was looking past myself and looking into my now eyes, I didn't see me. I stared deeply, desperately trying to solve my own mystery. For a minute, I forgot about the room, sleep, the drugs, my friend and everything, even those demon voices, that was trying to kill me. I'm just staring in the mirror looking at myself and didn't like what I was seeing. I began to get closer in the mirror, trying to see who it was inside me, because, I'm telling you, it was not me. Tears began to roll down my face as if it were on its own accord. I said to myself, "I can't do this anymore."

I dried my face and didn't have the answer but I just need a change in my life. I began to lay down on the bed, and my friend asked, " Are you ok?" "Yes, I'm good," I said, although I wasn't. Now I'm thinking, What was it that I saw in my eyes, when I looked into the mirror? My eyes are closed again, but this time I have a different feel about myself. I'm still wondering what was those choice of words said to me? "Day of salvation" what could it mean? I'm feeling enough peace and clam where I feel like I can go to sleep. I felt like I was just beginning to get some sleep when, I felt a vigorous tap on my shoulder and heard a voice at the same time say, "Get up, go to church, today is the day of salvation!"

 I jumped up this time for real, looking around, my heart was racing. I'm thinking, ghosts, demons or something? My, friend asked,"What's the matter?…What's wrong?"Did you hear that, did you feel that?"I asked."I didn't hear anything or felt anything, what are you talking about?"she said. I was definitely thinking, I'm tripping from these drugs, now I'm hearing voices , seeing things and feeling things. I need help. I ran to the bathroom and this time, I am really taking a look at myself. I wanted to see what I saw earlier. I really began to stare at myself in the mirror. I have never experience anything like this before. What is going on? I'm truly disturbed right now. I can still feel the fingers in my shoulders where, whatever touched me. I stayed in the bathroom trying make heads or tail from what was happening to me?

I went to talk to my friend and asked her if she didn't mind leaving? I felt bad, but I was going through something. She asked, "What's wrong, what's happening?" I said, " I need to go to church." "Go to church, She said," after all that we've been doing?""I know right! I can't explain right now, I just need to go,"I said. She got up and got herself together, I gave her the bathroom, and we made plans to meet later that evening. She had a friend her in the States from Switzerland,

and I assured her we would hook up and have a party. "So we'll talk later today," she said. "Sure thing,' I said.

I went back upstairs to jump in the shower and together dressed. I had so much running through my mind at the time. For some reason I was feeling nervous. I had not attended church in years, I didn't even know how to dress. My mind went all the way back to when I was a teen. I know I'm expected to wear a suit and tie. I'm in my room looking for a suit to wear and turned on the TV.

While looking in the closest, I heard this song. It made me stop everything and sit at the foot of the bed. I heard this angelic voice singing. This man was singing my life through song. I could hardly believe it! It was so orchestrated, I could hear sound all around me. I was looking around as if they were in my room right there with me, and I hear these words;

Straighten My Life Out (The Winans)
   Written and Lead vocals Marvin Winans

[Verse 1]
   I have to admit
   That I thought I had it under total control
   Feelings inside
   Seem to override what I know
   I'll take the blame
   And I feel quite ashamed
   That I let it go this far
   But I'm coming to You (Coming to You)
   Honest and true (Honest and true)
   Telling you
   Do what you have to for I

[Chorus]
   I don't wanna love wrong
   I don't wanna see wrong
   I don't wanna be wrong
   So straighten my life out again
   (Do it again, yeah)
   Straighten my life again

[Verse 2]

Now, believe me I've learned
And the greatest concerns is
That it never happens again
So here's where it ends (Here's where it ends)
I'm making amends (Making amends)
I lived that way once
I can't live that way again

[Chorus]
I don't wanna love wrong
I don't wanna see wrong, no, no
I don't wanna be wrong
So straighten my life out again
(Oh, oh, do it again)
Could you just straighten my life out again

[Bridge]
You said you could make the crooked straight
And in the middle of a desert
You could spring a well
So what I'm asking of You
Ain't hard for you to do
Would you just take my life, make it right
Turn this darkness into light

More
[Chorus]
For I just wanna love right, oh Lord
I just wanna see right, that's all it is
I just wanna be right
So straighten my life out again
(And do it again, do it again)
Would you please straighten my life out
For I, I just wanna love right
I, yeah, wanna be able to see you right
Oh, I wanna be right
So straighten my life out again

[Outro]
Please do it

Please do it for me, Jesus
Would you just straighten my life out
Straighten my life
Straighten my life
Straighten my life out
Straighten my life
Straighten my life
Straighten my life
Straighten my life
Straighten my life
Straighten my life out
Straighten my life
Straighten my life
Straighten my life
Straighten my life again
Straighten my life

The way they repeatedly said, "Straighten my life out," was tearing me apart! It's been many years ago and I can still feel The Holy Spirit in my hands as I'm typing this. Those brothers and *Bishop Marvin Winans* was instrumental in saving my life. God used them and Marvin directly through song. It was as though he laid hands on me. Around all of those drugs in my house and I had no desire to touch any of it after being ministered to in song. The lyrics preached to me, but Marvins delivery of the song, convicted me, not condemned me. *Thank you Brother Marvin,* also *Carvin, Michael and I salute my brother Ronald and Dad...Pop Winans*, they are in Heaven having themselves a good time, there are no words to express how much joy they are having all the time. He's "One of the One's Who Did." If I never get to see you here, I will get to see you home and tell you, " You may never know how many people you have reached?"

Now imagine hearing something like this, right after you hear, "Get up and go to church!" The lyrics were right on point and unbelievable. I was crying like a baby, I was in total disbelief. Really, I was crying after the song went off TV and was looking around, like, are you for real? Lest then two hours ago, I was holding my chest , thinking I'm having a heart attack and now this brother just took me to church in my bedroom.

It felt like my bedroom had become a sanctuary for God. I didn't want to hear nothing else on TV. I turned it off, still sobbing, because the way this man sang that song, from the depths of his heart and soul. He made me feel like I could go to God for anything. They (the Winans) helped me to have the courage to walk through that church door. Now I was dressed and ready.

I went to my car and had a dilemma, I don't what church to go to? First thought is the church I used to attend form the age of 11 years old, but I don't know what I would say? I was totally HIGH! Three days with no sleep, except, maybe the ten minutes I was trying to get earlier before God disturbed me. Sometimes, I would wonder, If in fact I would had an cardiac arrest trying to sleep? Only God knows! I truly believe that Good warns us and gives us a chance to reconcile to Him, but we have to make the choice. I chose to see the signs, hear the signs and believe the signs, and got up as I was instructed to do.

As I am driving, I hear within me a calm spirit of a voice telling me to go to my Family's church. I was thinking,"I don't want them to see me in this condition. I cleaned up pretty well, but three days, no sleep, constantly getting high. But, again, I am obeying the good voice, telling me to go to my family's church. When I arrived in the parking lot, I was shaking, I was so nervous. I'm thinking, what will they say, or think? Will they see in me that I saw in the bathroom at my house. Somehow, I feel different, ever since I heard that song, "Straighten My Life Out."

I parked the car and here goes. I'm walking up the steps and approaching the front door. I can see some people, but mainly two people ready to open the door to greet me. To my surprise, one of the gentlemen to speak to me was an usher. He was dressed in a suit and had white gloves on and very polite to me. He said, " What are you doing here this morning?" I was shocked! I asked him what was he doing in church and not just that, but working as an usher? He said, "I've been here for over three years now and I have been cleaned from drugs." Then he said, "Man I can't believe you are in church and I am going to take you to the front to be seated." Then I responded "Whatever." He replied by asking "Where would you like to be seated?" My response was "It does not matter."

As we began to walk down the aisle to where I was to be seated the pastor was already preaching and I heard the Bible close (slam shut via the mic) and the pastor said, **"God, just changed my message, TODAY is the day of salvation for someone that is here."** Then to my surprise this was the third time I heard that phrase in one morning. When I sat in my seat I couldn't help but to feel that God was giving me signs. The pastor began to preach about Jesus Christ, his love for people, why he came, why he died and that God loves you no matter where you come from. The message was mainly about the Love of God and that you could come to him with any problems you have.

I could not believe that I was actually in church and it was Easter Sunday. When the pastor started to speak about how the tomb was empty that Jesus had been buried in and that he had risen and came to life. And because Jesus live we can live. Just as he rose we can rise above any circumstances in our lives. The pastor proceeded to come down from the pulpit toward the main floor as she continued to speak. She was walking the aisles while preaching and it was my life that she was talking about and that really caught my attention. She was not looking at me but still as she spoke she was talking about my life and there were things that only God could know.

I couldn't help but feel that my whole morning was orchestrated and planned out somehow. I began to feel nervous for some reason and did not understand the reason why at the time. The more she spoke the more my life was being revealed to me. Afterwards, she made an altar call and asked if anyone needed to give their life to the Lord. Then I really became nervous because I wanted to go and get prayer but I felt ashamed due to the fact that I was high for three days. People started to walk toward the altar for prayer and all of sudden I became severely nervous. I began to hear voices, the same voices that were talking to me telling me to continue to smoke the cocaine.

They were trying to talk me out of going up to the altar and get prayer and for some reason I could not move, I felt paralyzed. As the pastor was praying for other people she continued speaking and asking is there someone else that needs prayer? And as I was looking the altar was full and people were in line. A brother from the church tapped me and asked me "Brother, would you like to come up with me to get prayer?" And I replied "No, I am good." Even thought I wanted to go and he replied " Are you sure?" and I responded "Yes." I put my head down as if I could side my shame because that is how I felt. I began to feel that all eyes were on me but that was not necessarily true.

I started to think maybe I am paranoid so I kept my head down for a minute and between the prayers the pastor kept saying, "Someone else needs to come up here for prayer." That caused me to look up to see if the prayer line was shorter and I saw the brother in line that asked me to go up with him to get prayer. Then the pastor said it again, "Someone else needs to come up here for prayer." And when I looked to my surprise it was still a long line and I asked myself Why does she continue to ask that someone else needs to come up for prayer as there seemed to be plenty people to pray over. She prayed for some people but in between the prayers she spoke some more personal stuff that aligned with my life that only God knew.

At that time, I asked God for a sign because I wanted to be sure. I began to talk to God and I say "If that same brother that came earlier asks me again if I would like to go up there to get prayer then Lord, I would go." When I looked up from praying, the same brother had four people ahead of him before his turn for getting prayer. Then all of a sudden he got out of line and I was thinking he got a call and stepped out of the line. He moved to the side of the church going toward the back and then I didn't follow him as far as looking. Seemly, out of nowhere the same brother was excusing himself from several people as he was walking toward where I was seated. He came straight to me and asked "Brother, Are you sure you do not want to go up here and get prayer with me?". At that moment I responded "Yes" and he looked surprised. I immediately got up and followed him to the prayer line. It felt really awkward going up for prayer because I grow up in church and I was always on the other end of stuff.

I used to be the musician that would play the music for altar calls while people were getting prayer so this felt really strange. The brother was in front of me and it was his turn for prayer. I was behind him and as he was getting prayed for my heart was pounding really hard because I knew I was next. Now, it was my turn. The big moment because I asked God for a sign. When I stood there before the pastor she just starring at me without saying a word, it almost appeared as if she was looking into my eyes like into my soul like the way I was looking at myself int he mirror when I was home. Then she tapped me in my chest toward my heart and she said "God, said you can't fix it. He is going to fix it."

And let me tell you that shocked me because when I was standing in line waiting for my turn I was negotiating with God in my heart. I said to the lord within myself , "if you give me two to three months to go to the streets and handle my business and take care of any debts that is related to the drug dealing I promise you I would come back here and I will give you my life." When the pastor tapped me in my heart and said what she said about I could not fix it that God had to fix it, that is what shocked me because how would she know that I was asking God within myself for time to fix somethings. Then she proceeded to say **"God just told me that TODAY is the day of salvation for you."** WOW! Now, this was the fourth time I heard this same phrase in one day. At that point I just surrendered and said "OK, Lord, I am here."

The pastor looked and asked me, "Do you want to be saved" and I replied "Yes." And she said "Ok, lift up both of your hands and I want you to call on the name JESUS while we pray for you and close your eyes." I began to call on the name of JESUS repeatedly while they were praying for me and then I heard her say call him louder and I was feeling a little embarrassed because I was still high. Though I was feeling reluctant I just complied and I began to call on the name of the Lord and the more I called on him the freer I began to feel. I do not know what happened but all of a sudden I was feeling bold. And I began to call on him louder and the pastor said, " That's it, call him." As I was saying Jesus over and over I started to choke and I started to cough and the pastor said "do not stop, keep calling him" and I did.

 I began to push through whatever it is I was going through. I felt my mouth getting dried and I started to feel nausea. Then I could taste cocaine in my mouth as if I was eating some and it was bitter…very bitter. With all of this taking place I was still calling on the name of Jesus because the pastor kept saying " Do not stop calling on him." I was starting to struggle within myself saying how can I continue to call Jesus while I am choking but I continued to call him anyway.

All of sudden I could smell cocaine like it was being cooked on a stove. The bitterness and taste hit the pit of my stomach and just for a moment I felt so sick it was almost unbearable. I was tempted to quit and go sit down. I was tired, I felt drained, I was remembering I was up for three days and three nights without any sleep. Just when I was about to quit I heard the pastor say "It is right there, do not quit, keep calling him." So I did. I kept calling on the name of Jesus. T I felt it when it came out of me and it felt like I was vomiting but I was afraid to open my eyes and they kept saying call on the name of Jesus. And just like that, I was no longer feeling sick, I was not tired but got a renewed strength and I kept calling on the name of the Lord. I could hear people praying around me but at the same time I could hear God speaking within me. He said "How can you crave for a hamburger if you never tasted one?"

The devil introduced you to the taste of cocaine like the mother would introduce a new taste of food to her child. Then he proceeded to say " I am going to take the taste out of your mouth." Then I felt as if someone's hand reached down into my belly and pulled out everything that was in me that was making me sick. I heard him say " I have called you and anointed you to work for me." And I heard myself speaking another language I did not know to myself. I thought I was still calling on the name of Jesus but I was told after the fact that this went on for about an hour and half but to me it seemed as minutes.

When it was all said and done and I opened my eyes most of the people from the service were gone. Everything looked new, bright, I felt light on my feet and I didn't know what to think or what I was suppose to feel since I was not sure of what happened. There were ministers and pastors asking me how I did I feel? So I looked around and I did not know how to quite make out of what I was seeing and people were excited for me. I rushed to leave to try to put together in my head what just took place. But I left feeling brand new. I did not feel the same. As I was leaving someone asked , Do you have a Bible?" and I replied "No."

During my ride home, I was talking to God but he was not talking back to me but I felt excited, felt joy and peace. I went straight home. I could not wait to get in my house to take it all in without an audience. As soon as I walked through the front door I closed it behind me, shut it and locked it as if I was running from something. As soon , I took a sigh of relief of being home I felt like

* * *

I wanted to rest. All of sudden God started talking to me and I could hear him clearly giving me instructions. He said "Now, I have cleaned you up and I want you to clean your house." Give rid of your bar, the liquor, cocaine, weed, scales all of those things that were ungodly he instructed me to trash it and I had the energy to do it. I began to bag everything up , being that I as a contractor I had a dump truck in the back of my yard. I threw everything on the back of that truck. I flushed the cocaine and drugs down the toilet.

Afterwards, I felt I could rest as I felt God had given me those instructions and I obeyed. I felt peace and all I wanted to do at this point was to get in the bed and go to sleep. But the I remembered that I had made a date with my two friends for that evening. I knew I would not know what to say to them as I was still processing what took place. I went to "Do Not Disturb" with all my devices. I laid down and I had the best sleep that I have not had in some years. Just as I felt a tap on my shoulders earlier that morning I felt that again but now the voice said " Go back to that same church and tell them what the lord has done for you" When I got up it was already after 7pm and I was wondering if the church had service at that time. Without knowing, I got myself together and headed that way and I had a thought when was the last time I had something to eat because I was not hungry.

I proceeded to the church and they were having service. When I walked through the door al ot of people were excited to see me and I was surprised. When the pastor saw me she said " We were just talking about you and wondering how you are doing." She was about to go preach and was on the microphone and she asked me " do you have something to say" and I was nervous but replied "Yes."

When I stood in front of all those people I felt intimidated. I began to tell them how I was a drug addict, a drug dealer and all of the things that happened that morning that compelled me to go that church. I told them how in prayer and during service the pastor was preaching was my life and she did not know it. The life style, the girls, the drugs, the clubs, the money but after that you do not have any peace. There was so much rejoicing and the glory of God filled the place that the pastor did not get to preach. We just celebrated. I had so many people congratulating me and welcoming me into the church. That was the beginning of my journey.

* * *

I did not realize that earlier that day that demons were cast out of me. When God snatched all that out of me at that time I did not know it was demons spirits. From that day forward I never did drugs again, never got high and never got drunk to this day. God totally delivered and rescued me. So I am a living witness that God is real and the power of him delivering and saving is real. This morning started out being my worst day and by the night I am saying it turned out to be my best day.

Through this I began to understand that God had called me and anointed me for people who are addicted, oppressed, possessed and in need of God's love and power.   I am not someone to judge and condemn since I could never judge anyone who battles with addiction because of what I have gone through.

So, this is my gift and miracle…MY RESURRECTION. I am sharing with you, because, if he did it for me, he can do it for you, because God is no respect of persons. This is my true testimony of the Lord Jesus Christ. He IS RISEN! Jesus is alive and well.

God was gracious and merciful to give me my gift and miracle this **Easter Morning**.

CHAPTER SEVEN

Life After

I found myself in the courtyard and have no clue as to how I got there. Its beauty is beyond any words to describe. As far as my eyes could see, was a "picture perfect" landscape. Then there was a fence, maybe setting parameters. This fence was sitting on a foundation of gold for the footer. The purest gold ever seen, it looked almost like gelatin, it was so clear.

The fence was tall in statue and wide but above all it was not regular stones or any masonry like materials. They were the size of boulders, not anything set by hands like a bricklayer or stonemason...they were huge! Amazingly the stones in the wall were like what we have as jewelry. They were diamond, jasper, ruby, sapphire, emerald, onyx, and others that I personally could not identify but you know that they were precious and very expensive stones.

I was filled with such completeness like I've never felt before. It was different, nothing like what I was accustomed to in the earth, nothing could compared to this. I was thinking, who is this God to have designed a wall with such unprecedented unique beauty. Again I'm thinking this is His fence, similar to a property line. Wow! As I stood gazing in aww, I heard a voice say, "You are a man of numbers, give me an estimate on its cost." I was astonished and impressed to hear this especially in a place like this. I'm also thinking, who knows I'm a man of numbers? I'm a General Contractor and Estimator by profession and not understanding numbers and cost would be detrimental to my life. I'm still adjusting to this place, that's the reality of this experience.

I knew I was there but, it was not made plain to me exactly where

I was. You just instinctively knew it was heaven. So I'm standing there staring at the task set before me. I'm thinking to myself that I will need a pad, pencil and calculator. Before I could speak, to make my request known, the pad, pencil and calculator appeared in my hands. I was astonished like before, when I was at the dinner table, but this time I don't see anyone to assist me. I'm feeling relieved, I have what I need to put together the cost of this fence and began to work the numbers.

In my profession, in order to put together an estimate, you must know the material cost and quantities, then labor. These three factors are a must, in order to achieve a price. The formula of square feet, square yards, cubic feet, cubic yards and linear feet are those most commonly used for this type of estimate. I now proceed, thinking I have everything I need to achieve this task.

I started to access the materials to put together the price. Very quickly to my surprise a reality check happens and I realize that these materials are not the norm. Starting with the footers, they are pure gold. Well, no gold is equal this gold known to man on the earth. Now I am troubled, because I know without the information of where the gold comes from and its unit cost, I can't move forward on this.

I'm looking at the fence's length, width and height and as a professional I am troubled. I don't want to be a disappointment to God by saying I'm unable to perform this task. With a heavy heart, I spoke out to Him with such caution because I don't know how He's going to receive what I have to say. I'm now thinking as well, was I too confident in my experience and ability. I said, Lord, this fence is so long and tall, I don't know. Before I could finish my sentence to express my dilemma, He reached out His hand and pointed towards the fence.

A light came from His finger like a laser and cut two lines and made a section, similar to control joints. The section now was about 40 feet long and 40 feet in height (all things are possible in this world). Now I was feeling relieved that I did not have to tell Him I was having difficulties with the calculations. I proceeded on with my calculations and ran into another challenge. The thought of these types of materials and their value, were running the numbers off of the calculator.

Where can I find gold so pure and diamonds by the tons when we the usual measures are by carats? I'm having actual and literal thoughts of even mobilization of said materials. "The cost is going through the roof", as they say in the construction industry. The materials alone are price- less! With great reluctance and somewhat disappointment I expressed to the Lord that I could not give a price, because the value of the materials alone are greater than all of the wealth probably in the earth.

He had already begun to move as if to exit the garden, then said to me, "I AM going to bless you, according to "My" riches and glory! Then He took a brief pause as He was leaving and looked back at me, as I was looking at him in total shock. He said, "Oh, you haven't even been to my house yet." Then He left and you could see the glory of His light gradually leave my presence. I realized at that moment, that rewards are inevitable after death. Apostle Paul talked about receiving a crown and rewards. Life is a continuation not the end. Maybe the end of time but not life or eternity.

I was totally beside myself with shock and excitement to hear these words. I'm also astonished thinking; does God have personality, was that a little humor with this statement? I took that as to imply, the house held more valuables than the Courtyard...wow! My blessings are coming from a source where there is no scarceness. In this place everything is done with a spoken word. I have yet to see something done by hands. God's word is almost like seed sown into soil to produce fruit or like the seed of a man placed into a woman and a child is conceived.

I am so moved right now by the reality of this place... it's real! When most people die or are about to die they talk of a better place. What place are they speaking about? Is it made up or imaginary or could it be that the part of them that was created by the Creator, who is call- ing them home. Maybe the spirit in them desires to go back to where it originated. As I stand here in total bliss, I find myself drifting almost as in a dream.

I hear a voice and am wondering who it is and where I am going. I found myself lowering to the earth. I could see the earth and came through clouds. All of a sudden I could see communities as if I was on a plane or helicopter. I then proceed without any control, down into my house roof, now I was back into my bedroom. I looked at my body on my bed. I walked over to the bed and laid down into my body as if I was lying on top of myself.

As I lay down, I realized that this is my soul and now it has become one with my body I popped up, gasping for air, my heart was racing like crazy. I jumped up and I was afraid, because I realized I really was gone to heaven, a whole other world! I will never be the same again. I had a visit with God and eternity. We all are given a space in time but the real life, in the Universe, Heaven. Heaven is so beautiful! Why look at the stars if we don't believe life is bigger than life? How arrogant of us to live on a planet in which appears to be the only one depended on gravity and air to live. We live here on earth by the rule of "Majority wins" even in our voting system. Well, the entire universes out numbers us...no challenge, hands down! Are we deceived to believe we are the majority? I say, there is life after this...

God is so real, Jesus is real, HolySpirit is real! We read about people in the Bible having encounters with angels, but when someone of today's time talk about their encounters, people think, "Crazy!" Mary told of her experience even to the point of being pregnant. Question: are these so called angels gone, dead, retired or what... where are they? I know they are real. We have bought into the lazy way of believing...Rest.

Let the ones of the old be the encounters, while this generation is too intelligent or evil too evil to believe. I don't want to hear another person talking about heaven but don't believe someone can have the same experiences they preach and write books about. You may have studied God's word, but you need to experience God's Word!

Information verses revelation. You have knowledge and information (Degrees) but have no revelation. You have to spend more time with God than your books. Every great person we preach about in the Bible have had some kind of divine encounter. So is God dead? Is he retired? Is Jesus alive and Limited? He said, no doubt you will see angels sending and descending upon the Son of Man.

Angels are our servants. They are waiting on instructions! Leave religion and tradition. So what's suppose, to happen, are we to not believe in them on earth, then have a sudden change of heart and mind when we get to heaven, or do you really believe there is a heaven? We as the church must make up our minds and Theology. If it's not real, then this is a HUSTLE! I'm a whistle blower, I would be the first to educate people to run and keep their money, families and time to themselves.

Read God's Word people for yourself. Spend time with God, and He will share secrets of the kingdom with you! If a pastor preaches every week out of the Bible, but don't believe the same Bible they preach/teach out of, then...RUN!

The Apostle Paul in his writing you can hear his growth and maturity in God. He spoke of his encounter and wasn't sure what was happening to him. He understands scripture makes it plain, that flesh and blood cannot inherit the kingdom of God, meaning, This present body cannot live in heaven's environment, for example we can't breath or survive outside of earth's atmosphere.

"I must go on boasting. Although there is nothing to be gained, I will go on to visions and revelations from the Lord. I know a man in Christ who fourteen years ago was caught up to the third heaven. Whether it was in the body or out of the body I do not know—God knows.

And I know that this man—whether in the body or apart from the body I do not know, but God knows— was caught up to paradise and heard inexpressible things, things that no one is permitted to tell. I will boast about a man like that, but I will not boast about myself, except about my weaknesses.

Even if I should choose to boast, I would not be a fool, because I would be speaking the truth. But I refrain, so no one will think more of me than is warranted by what I do or say, or because of these surpassingly great revelations. Therefore, in order to keep me from becoming conceited, I was given a thorn in my flesh, a messenger of Satan, to torment me. Three times I pleaded with the Lord to take it away from me. But he said to me, "My grace is sufficient for you, for my power is made perfect in weakness."

Therefore I will boast all the more gladly about my weaknesses, so that Christ's power may rest on me. That is why, for Christ's sake, I delight in weaknesses, in insults, in hardships, in persecutions, in difficulties. For when I am weak, then I am strong." (2 Corinthians 12:1-10)

Paul says, "It was unlawful to even speak of the things he saw" well now it's LAWFUL! This generation is the most knowledgeable in all history. At Jesus return, he is not eager to punish those who sought him and he shared some things in advance in which we are going to see anyway. I'm confident aster all of my suffering, that it's time for the world to know. Get ready church for miracle, signs and wonders, but just as equally to that, get ready for the revealing of the anti-Christ!

Oh yes…there's "Life After Death" because all of them folks of God are elders and saints including the followers of Christ who were persecuted. Those who apposed God is being punished. Their future to us ,is the present to them. They are there right now. Paul knows it is Lawful for this generation, to know some of the secret things of heaven. Because Paul made it, he lives there now and is cheering for all of us as believers and the church of Christ.

Listen to what Jesus had to say about secrets of the kingdom of heaven,

"He replied, "Because the knowledge of the secrets of the kingdom of heaven has been given to you, but not to them. Whoever has will be given more, and they will have an abundance. Whoever does not have, even what they have will be taken from them. This is why I speak to them in parables:
"Though seeing, they do not see; though hearing, they do not hear or understand. In them is fulfilled the prophecy of Isaiah: " 'You will be ever hearing but never understanding; you will be ever seeing but never perceiving. For this people's heart has become calloused; they hardly hear with their ears, and they have closed their eyes.

Otherwise they might see with their eyes, hear with their ears, understand with their hearts and turn, and I would heal them.' But blessed are your eyes because they see, and your ears because they hear. For truly I tell you, many prophets and righteous people longed to see what you see but did not see it, and to hear what you hear but did not hear it." (Matthew 13:11-17)

"And he said unto me, These sayings are faithful and true: and the Lord God of the holy prophets sent his angel to shew unto his servants the things which must shortly be done. Behold, I come quickly: blessed is he that keeps the sayings of the prophecy of this book. And I John saw these things, and heard them. And when I had heard and seen, I fell down to worship before the feet of the angel which shewed me these things. Then saith he unto me, See thou do it not: for I am thy fellow servant, and of thy brethren the prophets, and of them which keep the sayings of this book: worship God."Revelation 22:6-9 KJV"

"The seventh angel sounded his trumpet, and there were loud voices in heaven, which said: "The kingdom of the world has become the kingdom of our Lord and of his Messiah, and he will reign for ever and ever." And the twenty-four elders, who were seated on their thrones before God, fell on their faces and worshiped God, saying: "We give thanks to you, Lord God Almighty, the One who is and who was, because you have taken your great power and have begun to reign.
The nations were angry, and your wrath has come. The time has come for judging the dead, and for rewarding your servants the prophets and your

people who revere your name, both great and small— and for destroying those who destroy the earth." Then God's temple in heaven was opened, and within his temple was seen the ark of his covenant. And there came flashes of lightning, rumblings, peals of thunder, an earthquake and a severe hailstorm."
Revelation 11:15-19 NIV

"Keep on loving one another as brothers and sisters. **Do not forget to show hospitality to strangers, for by so doing some people have shown hospitality to angels without knowing it.** *Continue to remember those in prison as if you were together with them in prison, and those who are mistreated as if you yourselves were suffering.*

Marriage should be honored by all, and the marriage bed kept pure, for God will judge the adulterer and all the sexually immoral. Keep your lives free from the love of money and be content with what you have, because God has said, "Never will I leave you; never will I forsake you." So we say with confidence, **"The Lord is my helper; I will not be afraid. What can mere mortals do to me?"**

Remember your leaders, who spoke the word of God to you. Consider the outcome of their way of life and imitate their faith. Do not be carried away by all kinds of strange teachings. It is good for our hearts to be strengthened by grace, not by eating ceremonial foods, which is of no benefit to those who do so. We have an altar from which those who minister at the tabernacle have no right to eat.

The high priest carries the blood of animals into the Most Holy Place as a sin offering, but the bodies are burned outside the camp. Let us, then, go to him outside the camp, bearing the disgrace he bore. **For here we do not have an enduring city, but we are looking for the city that is to come."**
Hebrews 13:1-7, 9-11, 13-14 NIV

"Then I saw a great white throne and him who was seated on it. The earth and the heavens fled from his presence, and there was no place for them. And I saw the dead, great and small, standing before the throne, and books were opened. Another book was opened, which is the book of life. The dead were judged according to what they had done as recorded in the books.

The sea gave up the dead that were in it, and death and Hell gave up the dead that were in them, **and each person was judged according to what they had done.** *Then death and Hell were thrown into the lake of fire. The lake of fire is the second death.* **Anyone whose name was not found written in the book of life was thrown into the lake of fire."** *Revelation*

20:11-15 NIV

"Just as people are destined to die once, and after that to face judgment, so Christ was sacrificed once to take away the sins of many; and he will appear a second time, not to bear sin, but to bring salvation to those who are waiting for him."Hebrews 9:27-28 NIV

...Oh yes...there is life after death...

CHAPTER EIGHT

Heaven The Place

I was in this place where there were Beings and Creators of all sorts, such as never seen before. There are some similarities as to the comparison of earth but still different somehow. It is a beautiful place. I couldn't help but wonder, if I was dreaming? This place has no time, because its eternity. Everything in time as we know it came from here. Time is like a capsule, a "module" a piece, taken from this place. Time serves a purpose, it is the space where we are evaluated concerning the heart, whether it is with good or evil intent? Everything we see here is alive and nothing's dead. Death has no place here...it cannot be explained, but you can feel the life. There's no threat to it anywhere.

They have the essentials for life as we do but without the toiling and despair. In this place there is no indication of gender as we know it, but characteristics, authorities and positions of responsibilities. Being that I have knowledge of where I come from, the earth is always before me and in my mind. I cannot help but to compare my knowledge to theirs.

Based upon my experience in the world where I come from, I see duties performed by beings that would be probably female, but again they have no sexual organs for the determination of separating them by gender, but somehow you know by their characteristics and mannerisms. Life here is not produced by mating or giving birth, but by spoken word, it's the life giving method here. It's so peaceful and pleasant, such as I've never known before. I can't help but wonder, why am I here?

Why am I not received or rejected, just obviously permitted to be here, for now, because of whatever reason? I'm allowed somehow to be here but no one is acknowledging that I am here or do they even see me? Regardless of the circumstances, I feel the love here. Love is in everything and every being; No division, no strife, just unity and harmony, what a place. I don't think that I'm a spirit, because I I'm walking, not floating; also I have substance. There is such beauty here like nothing ever seen before. Everything is so absolutely beautiful, including the very atmosphere itself! There is a presence that can't be explained, only experienced. Everything appears to be perfect—What is this place?

Everyone is moving with purpose. I see them moving with diligence about what they do but somehow I don't see exactly what they are doing and yet they are not hid-ing anything. It's just that I don't understand what it is that they do, and how it works, but they are pleasantly diligent about it. There is one being in particular who stands out even in the midst of all surrounding beauty, this being is obviously in charge. Its very presence demands attention, praise and worship without even opening its mouth. The beauty of this being is like no other. This is obviously God's greatest display of His creative genius. This being is the most loved and has the greatest gifts and talents.

There is nothing to be desired, it has it all. When entering the room, everything changes, as if it was the rising of the sun. The presence is of great joy and peace. This being is well respected and loved.

The way it moves is similar to a mother taking care of her children but also like a wife preparing for her husband, having the authority of the house—at the same time like a CEO running a "Fortune 500" Corporation. With all of this, you still get the since that they are governed by something greater than what's seen. Everything is done with purpose and so organized—man this is impressive. This being is wearing a coat made of diamonds and it's almost like a king's robe but has a train like a wedding dress. It's like looking at a star with many stars...oh so pleasantly bright! There is a unity like never seen or revealed to mankind, greater than our greatest expectations.

Imagine having the closest family, the perfect marriage, the most obedient and disciplined children, the strongest army, the closest friend, the greatest award received, the best meal, the sweetest sweets, the best clothes, the most expensive jewelry, the highest academic achievements, the perfect body, the greatest health, the most handsome, the most beautiful, the biggest house, the best furniture, the most exotic car, the greatest wedding, the greatest honeymoon, the greatest song ever written, the best singer singing, the best dance, the best wine, the greatest sex, the greatest company, the purest love, the best singing, the greatest sport and the funniest comic, laughter is in the air and its everywhere— no sorrow, no pain , no death—just life everlasting......this is heaven, its perfect...what a place. This still serves no justice in description! I cannot explain this feeling that I feel, but it's real! It's like experiencing all of these joys at one time, but all the time. THERE'S NEVER A DULL MOMENT.

Somehow with all of this, it still feels innocent somehow. Every experience is like having mild to moderate orgasms and climaxes by just being there. I found myself walking through these palladium doors, they were huge... enormous! As I enter in, there's a long table already set with all kinds of food. I'm walking in but somehow it appears by my own thinking or even will and purpose. I'm wondering, why am I walking in uninvited? Somehow in my soul, I am guided, but very cautiously, I enter in, but do I take a seat? I see these beings that I assume are angels lined up against the wall, the full length of the table. The table somehow seems to be hundreds of feet long. I can't help but wonder who is this table set for? You can't even begin to imagine the stuff I am seeing. I've never seen anything like what I am experiencing. Amazingly, there are many simulations from the world where I come from, but not anything like this. As I look at these beings against the wall with their hands behind their backs and looking straight ahead. I'm looking to them since they are the only "living" in the room, for some kind of instructions or guidance.

They are standing at attention, almost with a military appeal but something about their eyes that are pleasant and peaceful...welcoming. I wanted to ask, if it was ok to have a seat but no one is there. Why am I the only one here? It had the quietness of a library, even much so, I did not want to speak aloud, feeling as though it would be out of order. I look to one being in particular for some type of assurance, to know if it was okay for me to be here.

Somehow without him speaking, his eyes gave me assurance that I'm in the right place. Now question, where do I sit? Or am I supposed to wait on other guests before sitting? I looked into his eyes and he stepped away from the wall with his hands still fixed behind his body, to my sudden surprise, a chair moves out from the table. I looked back at him in astonishment and without speaking from his mouth, he talked to me through his eyes or mind.

He was letting me know that it was my seat and proper place at the table. Soon as I stepped in front of the chair, the chair gently moved and slid me to the table. I then looked at him in astonishment, but he smiled with his eyes and stepped back into his place at the wall. I'm in total amazement! Now I still cannot get over the fact of this enormous table with all of this food and no one is here yet, but me. I'm thinking, who are the guests? All of a sudden I feel hunger but not as a pain from lack, but more of a desire to fill a void for my pleasure. The food looked perfect—I mean picture perfect! I can hardly wait! I dare not touch anything but had a thought of what I would like on my plate when it is time to eat. All of a sudden another being stepped from the wall just as the first one did before and food began to move as if it was an invisible person serving. Everything is moving with such poise and precision, it's most impressive.

I did not even have a chance to ask for anything, but everything I was thinking about and wanted went on my plate. I was looking at these beings with shock at the abilities of these wonderful creatures. They looked human but was very well built, large in size and height. After my unspoken request was filled, he then stepped back into position against the wall. I looked at him with thanks seemingly to communicate through my mind and eyes. They were very disciplined and professional. As I looked away from the being, all the others now had a look of welcome home and we are your servants—we're here to serve you.

When looking into their eyes, it was as though I could see worlds and experiences that transcends all time. Now they were all looking at me smiling, as the ability to smile with your eyes. Now I have a question, do I eat or do I wait? Who Am I waiting for? What Am I waiting for? Honestly, I don't even know. Suddenly everything changes. There's a great and blinding, but peaceful light at the end of the table. The distance and length of the table seems immeasurable. A voice starts to speak and it coming from the direction of the light. I am so comforted by this presence and voice, that I am speechless! He says to me, "Eat" somehow I collected myself to be able to eat what is on my plate. After the first bite, immediately tears falls from my eyes, down my face and I have no control. They were not tears of sorrow but of joy and wow, I am blown away by the taste.

What is this? This food is so indescribably delicious! There is nothing that I can compare, to describe its taste. Each bite, is like having any and everything great, as an experience, all happening at one time. All of this in food! Imagine all the pleasures of life, all wrapped up in one. He began to ask; why are you crying? I replied, I've never tasted or felt anything like this before and I am so glad that I made it! Amazingly, I had memory of my life on earth, but could feel no ills. I knew of my family, friends, my job, my address, my bank accounts, how much debt and my responsibilities. I could remember all of these things, but could not connect with pains, sorrows or disappointments. For some strange reason, I could not remember any bad things, as if they didn't matter or ever existed. I realized right then and there, that all the things we worry about and are concerned with, are a finished work with God.

Everything about me, felt like "me" but without the pain, worries, or concerns, even the thought of my children and their safety, was not a concern. You know by being here that life on earth is like a dream but this place is the reality! Whatever happens, you know it's already ok by design. I remember making an attempt to think of where are my children right now. I believed I was in real time. I was instantly relieved in knowing from within, that the worst thing to happen to them in time, or on the earth, would be the best thing to happen for them to get to eternity. It appears that all of this thinking started just by being in the presence of the Lord. He wasn't saying much by way of voice, but somehow I feel, He's responsible for the way my mind is all over the place. It's as though He allowed me to get all of those thoughts out of the way so we could move on. I felt such joy and peace as I've never experienced or imagined, while in the earth.

I don't have a mirror and didn't think to ask for one, but I'm almost sure, if I would have thought of it, surely it would have appeared, just as all the other times before. Now I'm thinking that I must have died to get here but have no recollection of dying or any related situations that may have contributed to the possibility of death. Anyway, I am happy that I made it! I'm so excited, I have the minimum of a billion questions to ask. Firstly I wanted to express my thanks for everything He's done for me and how elated I am to be here. His voice was so soothing and comforting, I did not feel fear at all but peace. Now that all of this is out of my mind, let me ask some questions! Before I could speak or even say a word, He began to tell me that my work was not finished in the earth. Immediately I began to cry as if by His words I had no choice. My tears now are of sorrow, because I don't want to go back to earth.

You would think that I would be happy to be with my loved ones and family, but to my surprise, I wanted to stay. I felt at home, like what home should be, nothing fake or pretentious, just pure love, safety and peace! He began to explain to me how my assignment was necessary and important. Somehow discerning that this was no debate, I calmed down and humbled myself to the reality of going back. I suddenly realized something; this whole table was set for just me and the Lord! Reality sets in because I know that I'm not dreaming but am in eternity! I thought about all the things at home on the earth and I tell you, it still was not enough to make me desire to go back. I had the comfort of knowing that everyone that I loved who was of the Lord, would make it here and nothing could stop that. I was comforted with that thought alone. I wish I could find the words to express and explain how it feels in this place but there are words to even come close. Somehow without saying, I can feel my time gently coming to an end for now.

I'm trying to encourage myself with the thought, I will return someday, but when? I'm reminded of an old saying, "Everyone wants to go to heaven, but no one wants to die."" I finished up my meal with conversation that I was not eager to hear. The Lord was giving me instructions of unfinished business in the earth that was assigned to me. Then I began to put fruit in my pockets and the funny thing is, I remember saying within myself; "I have pockets!" The fruit were going into my pockets! Then the Lord asked me, What are you doing? I said to Him, I'm taking this with me as evidence, because no one will ever believe me. The Lord replied, You don't need to take that with you. I said, but Lord, they will not believe me when I say that I have been with you and ate with you, unless I have some proof! What better proof than allowing them to taste some of what I HAD, then surely they cannot deny me.

The Lord then said to me; put the fruit back. I reluctantly put the fruit back on the plate. Then the Lord said to me; whenever you want to dine with me, just let me know. I immediately started crying like a child without shame. I expressed how much I didn't want to leave Him. He assured me that it was my destiny, it had to be fulfilled and everything will work out just fine. You must complete your work, He said. Leaving that room, I suddenly realized that I was a son not just a guest. The angels now had a smile on their faces as if to insure me that they were my servants and there to serve and assist. Somehow happy for me, at the thought of me finally knowing who AM, now I know that the work to be done was a divine order expected to be carried out in a kingdom way and fashion, because I am to represent God's way and they are assigned to help me. Wow! I have been granted access to heaven!

Another amazing thing is, I have recall and I know that I'm not worthy, but somehow justified! In a flash, I could see every mistake I'd ever done but now with a new meaning. I am supposed to use that as a template for grace and mercy founded by God's love for me, in return for all of us who would just hear His voice! I felt no condemnation but a responsibility to spread the good news and message. I found myself in another part of heaven where there was this great and beautiful being. This "Being"" was powerful just at its presence. It was worshipped and praised just the way we respond on earth to royalty or movie stars, singers, athletes, models, presidents...you get the picture.

Somehow, I'm feeling the origin of things...pure and uncut. The presence makes you feel beside yourself. This is definitely the place to be. Everything living knows this creature and honors it. I'm tempted to say, "He" but it's not gender, but state of being. Almost like it could be both wrapped up in one. It appeared somehow to represent every good gift and talent we would ever have and experience. Who is this? What is this? This Being was everything imaginable that is and was good. It somehow to me referenced everything in life that was desired to feel good. This Being no doubt is a god. What's amazing to me is the fact that I'm here but I'm not controlling anything, not my direction or even the place where I am? I don't know my way around but just appearing into places. I'm thinking... yes that's me—a thinker, why Am I allowed to be here?

The Being seemingly don't even know that I'm here. This Being was in charge. It appears to be the master of the, "Feel Good!"" Just its presence made you feel good. I was having multiple feel good experiences all in one just by being here. Like the feeling of the best of everything; from love of your life, to entertainment, you name it and it was here! The feeling of a show, the feeling of a concert, a best friend, a companion, a movie, a dinner, going out on the town, just everything good and pleasurable—it's too much to name—just everything good! Unlike the earth where I come from, nothing is forbidden. You can have your fill of pleasure...without condemnation. Without being taught I'm experiencing knowledge and it's blowing my mind. Somehow I know that everything experienced in the earth has a root and this is it. Wow it comes from this place. Everything is wonderful here, just great!

Everything we experience in this life is in relations to something in the afterlife which is really our before life. Every hurt and pain was before time, whether literally pierced or revealed until the day of piercing, but nonetheless, God went through it and felt every bit of it. When He said, "Man was made in His image and likeness,"" that's exactly what He meant from intellect and emotions—feelings! Our heart came from His heart, our ability to love comes from His love, our hurts was His hurts, our ability to dream and create stems from Him, our drive to live a good life, our love for the arts.

He is the greatest of all these things, because they all come from the very essence of who and what He is—and it goes on and on. He who loves life and also is the giver of that same life. God is and His very existence is beyond comprehension. Look at all of the beauty around us...it's Him; The colors, landscapes, the mountains, the ocean, sunrise and sun sets...it's all Him!

The moon and stars at night, the feeling when you find the right partner and lover in life, it's Him! Imagine all of these things without the drama, without death, without fear, without betrayal, without chaos, without sickness, without decease, without loss of any kind, without limits! Now that's HEAVEN!

This was the norm for this place, eternity which cannot be measured with time...it just is! Now imagine heaven is like our world, but perfect—nothing is out of balance. God created it as we do building things to enjoy for our own pleasure and so did God do so first. Image building your dream home with no limits as to what you so desire within and out.

Completion has been a longtime coming, but it's finally here. Now it's time to enjoy the fruits of your labor. Everything is happy and joyful. Every being, every creature and everything is for God's enjoyment and what's so amazing, all of this is bringing Him pleasure and joy. He also created things to receive pleasure while giving pleasure, it is the goodness of God; the none ending cycle of life. The angels were created for a specific purpose; to serve. Whatever God needed, wanted or desired, it was and still is there to reciprocate. Angelic beings have been with God throughout eternity and we cannot measure or fathom that with our finite minds.

This is God's vision and how arrogant are we to not acknowledge this when no matter how educated, talented, wealthy or even beautiful and gifted, we have no control over how long we will live here and certainly will not take anything with us when we leave. It doesn't matter how fearful we are of death and the unknown, death is inevitable. It is the one thing that we all have in common on this earth, without prejudice.

We all come from someone and somewhere bigger than ourselves…remember that!

Having this out of body experience or encounter has really changed my perspective on so many things. I'm not interested in persuading anyone's religious beliefs, but addressing a real Master, Creator, God, Beings, a tangible Place and System, Government— Kingdom. It appears that everything as we know it, comes from this place or kingdom. All religions have some percentage of truth, but I'm talking about relationship!

"And he said unto me, These sayings are faithful and true: and the Lord God of the holy prophets *sent his angel to shew unto his servants the things which must shortly be done. Behold, I come quickly: blessed is he that keeps the sayings of the prophecy of this book. And I John saw these things, and heard them. And when I had heard and seen, I fell down to worship before the feet of the angel which shewed me these things. Then saith he unto me, See thou do it not: for I am thy fellow servant, and of thy brethren the prophets, and of them which keep the sayings of this book: worship God."* Revelation 22:6-9 KJV

"I want you to recall the words spoken in the past by the holy prophets and the command given by our Lord and Savior through your apostles. Above all, you must understand that in the last days scoffers will come, scoffing and following their own evil desires.

They will say, "Where is this 'coming' he promised? Ever since our ancestors died, everything goes on as it has since the beginning of creation." But they deliberately forget that long ago by God's word the heavens came into being and the earth was formed out of water and by water. By these waters also the world of that time was deluged and destroyed. By the same word the present heavens and earth are reserved for fire, being kept for the day of judgment and destruction of the ungodly.

But do not forget this one thing, dear friends: With the Lord a day is like a thousand years, and a thousand years are like a day. The Lord is not slow in keeping his promise, as some understand slowness. Instead he is patient with you, not wanting anyone to perish, but everyone to come to

repentance. But the day of the Lord will come like a thief.

The heavens will disappear with a roar; the elements will be destroyed by fire, and the earth and everything done in it will be laid bare. Since everything will be destroyed in this way, what kind of people ought you to be? You ought to live holy and godly lives as you look forward to the day of God and speed its coming. That day will bring about the destruction of the heavens by fire, and the elements will melt in the heat. But in keeping with his promise we are looking forward to a new heaven and a new earth, where righteousness dwells." 2 Peter 3:2-13 NIV

"And I saw a new heaven and a new earth: for the first heaven and the first earth were passed away; and there was no more sea. And I John saw the holy city, new Jerusalem, coming down from God out of heaven, prepared as a bride adorned for her husband. And I heard a great voice out of heaven saying, Behold, the tabernacle of God is with men, and he will dwell with them, and they shall be his people, and God himself shall be with them, and be their God.

And God shall wipe away all tears from their eyes; and there shall be no more death, neither sorrow, nor crying, neither shall there be any more pain: for the former things are passed away. And he that sat upon the throne said, Behold, I make all things new. And he said unto me, Write: for these words are true and faithful. And he said unto me, It is done. I am Alpha and Omega, the beginning and the end. I will give unto him that is athirst of the fountain of the water of life freely. He that overcomes shall inherit all things; and I will be his God, and he shall be my son."Revelation 21:1-7 KJV

Jesus is resurrected and is seating in heavenly places right now as we speak. Why do we insist upon waiting to die to find out if he has risen and or is real? Once Jesus finished his work and dining on the cross, he went into the lower parts of the earth. He defeated death, hell and the grave, collected the keys from the enemy, and then set the captives free.

I have experienced a kingdom, which is very well organized and established. No sickness, or poverty, no sadness or fear...just life more beautiful and peaceful than any depiction known in our world This is the place!

So, where did **REST IN PEACE (R.I.P.)** come from?

CHAPTER NINE

R.I.P.

R.I.P. "Rest In Peace"
how often have we heard this?" Where did RIP come from?

The phrase was first found on tombstones some time before the fifth century. It became ubiquitous on the tombs of Christians in the 18th century, and for High Church Anglicans, Methodists, as well as Roman Catholics in particular, it was a prayerful request that their soul should find peace in the afterlife.

RIP, an acronym for "Rest in Peace," is a common condolence at funerals and a general response to someone's death. But RIP has also become a pop culture catch phrase with many different connotations. Though the term occasionally drifts from its original use, RIP is still widely used in conversation when someone has passed away. Secularly, it communicates a general respect for the one whom has died and condolence for friends and relatives who were close to that person. For Christians, we are reminded of the peace God brings from the pain of death for those who follow Christ. "There is no 'R.I.P.' without the Resurrected Jesus Christ, because he is the RESURRECTION!

The phrase began as a prayer, wishing those who died had found right standing with God, and were now resting eternally with Him. According to dictionary.com, "The Latin phrase (as requiescat in pace) began appearing on Christian gravestones in the 8th century, and became widespread on Christian grave markers by the 18th century.

* * *

"Biblical roots of "rest in peace" appear in Isaiah 57:2: "He enters into peace; They rest in their beds, Each one who walked in his upright way." (NASB) This verse is promising relief in death, an "escape from turmoil" this was their blessed hope. Isaiah is giving his account of what happens after we die under the Law.

"There was a certain rich man, which was clothed in purple and fine linen, and fared sumptuously every day: And there was a certain beggar named Lazarus, which was laid at his gate, full of sores, and desiring to be fed with the crumbs which fell from the rich man's table: moreover the dogs came and licked his sores.

And it came to pass, that the beggar died, and was carried by the angels into Abraham's bosom: the rich man also died, and was buried; And in hell he lift up his eyes, being in torments, and sees Abraham afar off, and Lazarus in his bosom. And he cried and said, Father Abraham, have mercy on me, and send Lazarus, that he may dip the tip of his finger in water, and cool my tongue; for I am tormented in this flame.

But Abraham said, Son, remember that you in your lifetime received good things, and likewise Lazarus evil things: but now he is comforted, and you are tormented. And beside all this, between us and you there is a great gulf fixed: so that they which would pass from hence to you cannot; neither can they pass to us, that would come from there. Then he said, I pray you therefore, father, that you would send him to my father's house:

For I have five brothers; that he may testify to them, lest they also come into this place of torment. Abraham said to him, They have Moses and the prophets; let them hear them. And he said, No, father Abraham: but if one went to them from the dead, they will repent.

And he said to him, If they hear not Moses and the prophets, neither will they be persuaded, though one rose from the dead," says, Jesus, who is The Resurrection.

Jesus said this before he was crucified, but knows it coming, just as he knows that he came to die. This man, son of God, God manifested in the flesh understood and understands death. He came to defeat death, awaiting his encounter and bout with death, hell and the grave. After the fact we find his account of winning. He gives us an inside of what happens when one dies right or wrong, good or evil. Listen to the dialogue taking place after death. Who's resting or who's not? We have been made to think death is final, but, instead it is the final enemy we have to fight through the victorious fight of Jesus. We have already won but we still have to fight so the enemy knows he can't ever bully us again. If you make it to Heaven you will have some dignity to know how to faced death and win. Jesus defeated this bully, but we are called to face him because he has won so many battles until Jesus beat the unholy crap out him. We are just like Jesus…victorious even in death.

We have Hades and Hell—the underworld. It's Paradise or Hell. Whatever the account, it's a holding place until the fulfillment of the prophecies of the long awaited Messiah which was and is to come, who is our Lord Jesus. When the prophet Isaiah spoke these things, he was awaiting the coming of the Messiah just as everyone else who believed and died by faith. The Patriarchs of the Old Testament died in hopes of the Messiah remembering them and the life they lived in the earth, by attempting to keep the law(of Moses) as followers of God. Jesus came to fulfill that same law, not to destroy it. No man or person was able to keep all of the law which made our sins to remain forever before us, to remind us, of how we will always need something much greater than ourselves. This is why there was so much shedding of blood through the offerings of animals, especially sheep and lambs. These represent weak, gentle and innocent. So matter how people may make fun of you or mock you as a believer, weak will be saved and rewarded but the wicked will perish.

"Rest in the LORD, and wait patiently for him: fret not yourself because of him who prospers in his way, because of the man who brings wicked devices to pass.
Cease from anger, and forsake wrath: fret not yourself in any wise to do evil.
For evildoers shall be cut off: but those that wait on the LORD, they shall inherit the earth.
For yet a little while, and the wicked shall not be: yes, you shall diligently consider his place, and it shall not be. But the meek shall inherit the earth; and shall delight themselves in the abundance of peace.The wicked plots against the just, and gnashes on him with his teeth.
The LORD shall laugh at him: for he sees that his day is coming.The wicked have drawn out the sword, and have bent their bow, to cast down the poor and needy, and to slay such as be of upright conversation."
But the wicked shall perish, and the enemies of the LORD shall be as the fat

of lambs: they shall consume; into smoke shall they consume away. (Psalms 37:7-20)

I have seen the wicked in great power, and spreading himself like a green bay tree.

Yet he passed away, and, see, he was not: yes, I sought him, but he could not be found.

Mark the perfect man, and behold the upright: for the end of that man is peace.

But the transgressors shall be destroyed together: the end of the wicked shall be cut off.

But the salvation of the righteous is of the LORD: he is their strength in the time of trouble.

And the LORD shall help them, and deliver them: he shall deliver them from the wicked, and save them, because they trust in him. (Psalms 37:35-40)

If I shut up heaven that there be no rain, or if I command the locusts to devour the land, or if I send pestilence among my people; If my people, which are called by my name, shall humble themselves, and pray, and seek my face, and turn from their wicked ways; then will I hear from heaven, and will forgive their sin, and will heal their land. (2 Chronicles 7:14)

The heart is deceitful above all things, and desperately wicked: who can know it? I the LORD search the heart, I try the reins, even to give every man according to his ways, and according to the fruit of his doings. (Jeremiah 17:8,9)

We have a choice in this world and that's very important to know why? Choose good or evil, we will be judged for our choices. Do we think we are here to take up space and what we do doesn't matter...NO that is far from the truth?

One day we will give an account for what we do and what we believe. This is the reason why giving our heart to the Lord Jesus is so important. Salvation is the work of the heart. It's in the heart where we decide if we will do good or evil, give life or kill and take that life away. God sees all and will judge everything. Put your trust in the Lord, repent often and ask for forgiveness for known sins and unknown. Holy Spirit is our Helper and teacher. He is innocent and a witness to truth and will not lie. Holy Spirit is like and innocent child just speaking truth. For example when one says, "I wasn't home when you came by the house" and your child says, " Mama, yes you was home remember, you told me to keep quiet, we heard the door." The child is not telling on you but telling the truth as innocence.

This is one of the reasons in the Word Jesus says,*"Truly I say to you, All sins shall be forgiven to the sons of men, and blasphemies with which soever they shall blaspheme: But he that shall blaspheme against the Holy Ghost has never forgiveness, but is in danger of eternal damnation.*

Why do we lie to people? Their souls are at stake! So much is going on and we stand by as the Church and say nothing. We are responsible for telling the truth, not in self righteousness, but, in love. We are not to condemn, but do not to put our heads in the sand either. I've personally paid the price of truth, God is real in my life and some people want you to be who you were before Christ. In order to do that, I would have to silence the Spirit of God within to make the lie comfortable but Jesus started a movement. The true church is a movement and will be the greatest celebration in Heaven. Jesus death wasn't a fable, neither was his Resurrection, so why should the Gospel of the Kingdom, and or, death be? There is life after life...whether heaven or hell!

Jesus is our saving grace. All of the offerings that were given on behalf of man's transgressions were types and shadows of the real to come. Jesus is that REAL!

As Christians, we believe death is the beginning of eternal life in heaven with Jesus Christ, our Savior. Paul wrote in 2 Corinthians 5:8, *"We are confident, I say, and would prefer to be away from the body and at home with the Lord."* Resting in Peace or Resurrected In Power? If resurrected, we have work to do, Satan and his followers are to be tried and judged then put in chains! Are the wicked resting? What are we saying or believing? We can't be both. There has been to much evil and wicked committed in this earth for God to turn His head for unreported sins. Take the Plea! Admit to the crimes and throw yourself at the mercy of God's court.

I'm not looking forward to "RESTING IN PEACE" but the exact opposite. I'm looking forward to seeing the enemy that I couldn't see that is spirit, who was working through people and situations against my life and loved ones. " NO JUSTICE...NO PEACE!" Satan and his angels, demons, workers of evil that have destroyed so many lives. How ridiculous, even the wicked gets "Rest In Peace" on their grave stone. What a fantasy! After all the hell they raised, lives destroyed, lies told to build themselves up while tearing others down...please! Wake up Church! Come on believers, we are seeing prophecies being fulfilled right before our eyes.

We don't need another lie told to us by no one. We need to know the truth, it will set us free. People are hiding out because of the lies they've been told. I pray for our young people, they have to deal with so much more than we had to at their ages. More knowledge and greater access to information, but very little revelation. The Devil used the word of God against Jesus in the wilderness from a place of information, but Jesus blew him out the water with word and revelation. We are living in trying times in-which were prophesied long ago. " This know also, that in the last days perilous times will come." (2 Timothy 3:1)

Nothing is weak about our God, he's merciful because he loves his people. Unfortunately people rather believe the lies over the truth. If you are a unbeliever and reading this , I am so thankful because of the price I had to pay to write this and get it published. I hope you accept God's love and turn away from your wicked ways? I'm the set free person from drug addition and whatever my spiritual step father had me doing. That rights! Satan was my step dad, and he used me for his dirty work, so I'm here with a vengeance, not a person of the flesh, but spirit!

Give a person their flowers while they are living." For the most part we have good intentions. Do we give the flowers? Do they know we are wishing for them to REST? To lose someone you love and respect, what an empty and devastating feeling. The pain cannot be sufficiently expressed or explained. What consolation can you get, or where can it come from? Is it possible that anyone, someone can remotely know how you feel? This thing is on me every single day of my life. My loss is too great for me. It appears to be too much for me to handle.

I'm bereaved , I'm lost, I'm shocked even, at what has happen and how I feel. I toss and turn struggling to sleep. I'm crying at random and at unexpected times. I know death is a part of life, but somehow I didn't see it as a part of my life, at lease not now. But let's be real here, I've never been prepared for this loss. I didn't want to prepare for this loss. Why can't things remain the same, or go back to how things used to be. I miss them, I miss it, the way things used to be. This pain is like nothing I've ever felt before.

This experience is not anything I would ever pursue...not ever! Then I discovered that Rest In Peace is not the state of being Jesus said for us as believers. We have life to live, not sleeping or resting? Not to appear insensitive, because you get to hear my state of mind before I had revelation, information was tormenting. Revelations from God's Word as to the truth, brought me consolation. We are so blessed to know God, and If you don't know Him, then just do it! Get to know Him for yourself. Spending time with God will give you revelation and not just information.

Sometimes we die for memories. When it's all said and done, that all it will be without God to meet us on the other side.

Life's a wonder that always makes us wonder...Where are they now? Every person who ever lived on this earth, is living somewhere in eternity, right now. Enjoying living or tormented with terror...I mean everyone.

The church has to wake up! It's confusing to the secular world, if we don't know the difference, in Resting or Living? We are the light of the world. Life is light...death is darkness! Let Satan have his death, hell and the grave. We have no businesses as the church (blood bought believers) children of God, weeping like heathens with no hope!

Yes, we weep, "Jesus wept",but not because there was no hope. His weeping was out of the compassion and love he has for people, but also because he knew, no matter what he did, there would be those who will not believe, even when the Resurrection and life is right there in their face.

Church, we are the lights of the world. When we go funerals , we are to take life and light...not darkness and death. We are encourage as best as we can, give condolences and love. We all need the Lord.

Which one is it, Resting or Living? *Resting In Peace or Resurrected In Power?*

If Jesus were here on earth, would he be saying, "Rest In Peace" when someone has died ...NO, he would not, because He is The RESURRECTION and LIFE?

RESURRECTED IN POWER!

CHAPTER TEN

The Church

"Upon this rock I will build my Church; and the gates of hell shall not prevail against it."

The first shall be last, and the last shall be first. We need you Lord!

LOVE: God is love and love is God! *For God so loved the world, that he gave his only begotten Son, that whosoever believes in him should not perish, but have everlasting life. (John 3:16)*

The first church came from Jesus's love and blood, and it WASN"T a building! The church is alive and love, it cannot be shut down, closed or foreclosed, not as long God lives there,, because, we (His People) are the Church.

Jesus answered and said unto them, Destroy this temple, and in three days I will raise it up. (John 2:19)

Love is not a competition but a completion! Love gives, hates takes it away. Anything that you've truly loved, look back and see what took it away? From Adam and Eve, who lost their two sons, via hate. Cain was jealous of his younger brother Abel and killed him, when he could have loved and learned from him. God said to Cain, Why are you wroth? And why is your countenance fallen? If you do well, shall you not be accepted? And if you do not well, sin lies at the door. And to you shall be his desire, and you shall rule over him.

For this reason and example, it is dangerous to compete with siblings, family, friends, spouses...etc, because it's lethal. Cain didn't share with his brother how he felt, he just went after him over a misunderstanding. How many relationships have had toxic ends, because of misunderstandings and jealousy? The church is stuck rights now in many cases because of the same thing as Cain and Abel. Be honest, are you a Cain, or are you Able?

Why do we compete in ministry? I can admire you, learn from you, cheer you, support you, praise your accomplishments, but never envy you or be jealous of you. No one can be better at being you...but...you! We all have our own calling and contribution to make to this world, family and community.

This writing is mandated to the church of believers. Anyone can read this and see the example of the danger of competing with something you are called to complete. When the devil working through the serpent talked to Eve, he manipulated her into second questing who she was, to compete with herself, husband and God. Her decision carries power! Her unborn children were effected. Careering after a god, when she was a god already.

Relationships are not working and divorce is at its highest in human history because of the same tactics used in the beginning, but know we are "lovers of ourselves." Satan is a loser, who uses other people's stuff to look successful, because he lost his place, he's on a vengeance for humanity to lose their place with God...don't do it! Everything he presented to them in Genesis, was their own stuff. If you are interested with God's love, favor, paradise, given dominion over every living creature, and in addition to that, given the authority to name all the animals...you're already like God.

How do we think God would be pleased with us doing whatever we deemed necessary to gain power, position, money, attention and success when He is God over all? He desires for us to love one another. To love us as he has loved and loves us.

Do you know church that the world is not as impressed with our gifts as we think? What the world needs is LOVE, not another empty headed, egotistical church or don't know if, I'm a church person? Jesus died for the church (His People) not a building or buildings. It was well over a hundred years before there was a brick and mortar house of worship, or what we call church today. Replacing prayer for production, Jesus said, "PRAY!" *And he spoke a parable to them to this end, that men ought always to pray, and not faint (quit, give up) Luke 18:1.*

What kills me is, we have church people and leaders who preach Jesus but limit the works of him. When someone speak of heavenly and spiritual things, they are the first to cast doubt and unbelief. Do you believe the works of the cross or not? Do you believe that Jesus died for all sins, past, present and future, or not? God is a Spirit! Don't allow anyone who glorifies their flesh and gifts to cause you not to believe in heavenly things, because I will tell you a truth, you will leave this world one way or another, and if you don't believe heavenly things, hell is waiting to welcome you in. **Jesus is Lord,** to the glory of God, he's not trying to be, and neither is he waiting to be validated by flesh and blood!

Now believe that fact and truth, because it's an everlasting reality. If not, we'll see you after you die and see what happens (note read Revelation in it's entirety) it has all sought of solved mysteries. I've had pastors upset with me for teaching and reading fro the Book of Revelation. I believed in them and their callings, then questioned, would God be the one telling them not to read the book, and or teach from the book?

As believers, Revelation is your book, it was never meant for the ungodly or world. When it was translated, they were afraid to tamper with the book. It is a reveal book, meaning, it is the allowance of us to look behind the curtain or veil, seeing secrets revealed, but wrap into mysteries. Use your Holy Ghost to enjoy and appreciate what the Lord has done for us as his children. The other mind blowing thing is, many pastors leaders do not believe in angels, how can you preach, teach God's word to his people and rail on those who have had angelic encounters. Heaven's entire account is surrounded by the presence of angels.

Mary's own account is an angel visited her to announce the coming of Jesus, and she would have a son, through her womb, if there is no angel, there is No Christ? Joseph said, he never touched Mary?

Remember, I pray you, who ever perished, being innocent? Or where were the righteous cut off? (Job 4:7)

* * *

Put on the whole armor of God, that you may be able to stand against the wiles of the devil.

For we wrestle not against flesh and blood, but against principalities, against powers, against the rulers of the darkness of this world, against spiritual wickedness in high places.

Why take to you the whole armor of God, that you may be able to withstand in the evil day, and having done all, to stand. Stand therefore, having your loins girt about with truth, and having on the breastplate of righteousness; And your feet shod with the preparation of the gospel of peace;

Above all, taking the shield of faith, with which you shall be able to quench all the fiery darts of the wicked.

And take the helmet of salvation, and the sword of the Spirit, which is the word of God: Praying always with all prayer and supplication in the Spirit, and watching thereunto with all perseverance and supplication for all saints. (Ephesians 6:11-18)

And take heed to yourselves, lest at any time your hearts be overcharged with surfeiting, and drunkenness, and cares of this life, and so that day come on you unawares.

For as a snare shall it come on all them that dwell on the face of the whole earth.

Watch you therefore, and pray always, that you may be accounted worthy to escape all these things that shall come to pass, and to stand before the Son of man. (Luke 21:36)

We may look good and sound good, but, the world is dying because we are not good. Again, what the world needs is love.

If we have love, then we can choose who to give that love to?

LUST: The devil is lust and lust is the devil. Lust don't love anybody! It's selfish! It is never satisfied, it is brutally self absorbing but not self sufficient. It is like a thief. Lust will steal everything you have and go to its next victim, leaving you distressed. Jesus said, "The thief comes only to steal, kill and destroy; I have come that they may have life, and live it to the full" (John 10:10). Who is the thief? Who is they?

* * *

The thief is Satan, the devil. He uses people to destroy people. The thief is the one who comes into your life to take from you and is never satisfied. You will look around one day in amazing hurt and shame, wondering, when did this happen to me? Where are all of my things, my joy, my peace and all of the love I once had? What happened to me? Lust don't have love, it can't! It does not exists. Lust is a wicked spirit! It cares for no one but itself. It will use you and abuse you, then move on and come back for more if you let it...why...because it's lust...it is selfish! Love and lust does not belong together. Lust and lust can't stand each other as well.

We are living in prophetic days...end times. A time where flesh will go after more flesh and never can be satisfied or fulfilled. So the goal is to try out as much flesh as possible seeking to be satisfied. Problem; flesh gets old, it changes, gets tired and stinks if unattended. The deception is to go from one thing to another in false hope of being satisfied.

Do you know that when you love, that's a part of God in you loving. All things has a source and love's source is God. God is love. He is not trying to love—He is love. When we remotely begin to understand His love, we will live a much better and secured life, without fear. No matter what happens in this world, God loves His children. The only reason why the world has not yet been destroyed, is because love has not yet finished its assignment for mankind. Despite the myth, "We are all God's children" this is not true.

The devil has children too. God is love and His children were created from that same love. Love is patient, not necessarily stupid. Sometimes evil takes kindness for weakness when the truth of the matter is, it's the love of God and patients with an hope to save, not destroy. And that hope is my love for you. It will ultimately win over the hate? Will you choose God who loves you over the one who despises you, uses you, for their own gain and destroys your life? Hate is a thief! Hate is a killer! Hate is a liar! Hate is a cheater! Hate divides! If your house or relationship is divided...look around for hate and lust and you will find them. Love did not sabotage you or divorce you...hate did...lust did. Lust will find a replacement..but love will create an original.

Love cannot be replaced...only refined! No matter who you are and where you come form, God loves you. Only He can love you the way you need to be loved. When a man loves you, he only can truly love you if he loves God, then who will love you through him. Your love is from them…vice versa, your woman can only love you if she loves God. Without God, we can't trust it…the devil is wanting and waiting. He is so desperate.

It can take on many forms. In some cases it can tolerate you for an agenda. When it need something from you hate can be polite and even nice to you to get what it want. Hidden agendas happen everyday. Lives are destroyed everyday by someone you loved and trusted. It's not how good it started but how bad it ended. When people hate you because they could not control you or the outcome, it wasn't love. When things don't turnout the way they quite imagined, then they turn on you, this is not love.

Many relationships are arrangements not love, in it for now, but have no endurance for later. Who are you now, who will you be 20 years from now? We fail, because we don't believe in sacrifice before reward. Even the victory Jesus achieved, came through pain before pleasure, cross before crown, death before life. Faith is our equalizer. All of us have been blessed with a measure of faith, but how do we use it, are we willing to us it? Many things we want will only come by faith. The great about faith is, it's spiritual! There are things we need from God that can only be received or accomplished through faith…believing God for them. Love and faith are partners. Jesus was able to endure the shame, disgrace, mockery, lies, deception, beatings and death because of faith and love. No one could separate him from the love of his father, and the Father's love for him.

 Know this fact, you cannot make someone love you. No matter how much you give or do, without love, it will never be enough. When you're not able to produce for lust, it will leave and find someone or thing else. Look at what we have become. We loved when things were more of a simpler time. We are bombarded with so much lust and promiscuity, it's almost impossible to this generation to be faithful. Without God, how can we be? When we approach the altar, we need to be sure God is there, endorsing our union. Through faith in God and love for him and our partner, we make the convent, God knows it will be by love and faith we will keep them.

* * *

"Love never fails." So if it failed…it wasn't love. You don't use to love someone…either you love them or you don't…never did! This doesn't mean their won't be challenges and fights, but it simply means, love will always "weather the storm"…love will be the last one standing. This is what true love is…being ONE. Jesus said, "Me and my Father are one and the same." No ONE could ever separate them! Satan tried! The Pharisees tried! The sinners tried! Sin thought it could because Sin to God was like Kryptonite to Superman. Satan thought by sin it would cause separation? "And about the ninth hour Jesus cried with a loud voice, saying, Eli, Eli, lama sabachthani? That is to say, My God, my God, why have you forsaken me?" (Mathew 27:46)

Do you know that when you hate, that's a part of Satan in you hating. He is the original hater—the origin. This is why haters are going to hate, they are being like their father, the devil.

*But now you seek to kill me, a man that has told you the truth, which I have heard of God: Abraham did not do such things. You do the deeds of your father. Then said they to him, We are not born of fornication; we have one Father, even God. Jesus said unto them, If God were your Father, you would love me: for I proceeded forth and came from God; neither came I of myself, but he sent me. Why do you not understand my speech? Even, because you cannot hear my word. **You are of your father the devil, and the lusts of your father you will do.***

He was a murderer from the beginning, and abode not in the truth, because there is no truth in him. When he speaks a lie, he speaks of his own: for he is a liar, and the father of it. And because I tell you the truth, you believe me not. Which of you convicts me of sin? And if I say the truth, why do you not believe me? He that is of God hears God's words: you therefore hear them not, because you are not of God.

Then answered the Jews, and said unto him, Say we not well that you are a Samaritan, and have a demon? Jesus answered, I have not a demon; but I honor my Father, and you do dishonor me and I seek not my own glory: there is one that seeks and judges.

Verily, verily, I say unto you, If a man keeps my saying, he shall never see death. Then said the Jews unto him, Now we know that you have a demon. Abraham is dead, and the prophets; and you say, If a man keeps my saying, he shall never taste of death. Are you greater than our father Abraham, who is dead? and the prophets are dead: whom make you yourself? Jesus answered, If I honor myself, my honor is nothing: it is my Father that honors me; of whom you say, that he is your God: Yet you have not known him; but I know him: and if I should say, I know him not, I shall be a liar like unto you: but I know him, and keep his saying.

Your father Abraham rejoiced to see my day: and he saw it, and was glad. Then said the Jews unto him, You are not yet fifty years old, and have you seen Abraham? Jesus said unto them, Verily, verily, I say unto you, Before Abraham was, I am. Then took they up stones to cast at him: but Jesus hid himself, and went out of the temple, going through the midst of them, and so passed by.
(John 8:40-59)

Although the Pharisee and Sadducees were the elite priesthood, they had a lot of issues. Because of their statue and wealth, they could hide them behind money and prestige, until Jesus came along. When people saw how connected Jesus was to the people, they started to realize, they didn't have a shepherd over them at all, they had masters. They were accustomed to the rich having access to everything first and the poor getting what was left, or what ever they could afford.

The Pharisees were accustomed to the VIP lifestyle and then Jesus comes along teaching, "He who is first, must be last and he who is last, must now be first. It's better to give than receive." Over turning tables in the Temple and driving out the money exchangers and reminding them of his Father's house, being a house of prayer. "You have turn it into a den of thieves!" What! He shifted the whole dynamic by his teachings of faith and trusting God for absolutely everything!

The religious leaders had people believing they were special and if you didn't get your treasure here on earth, you've lost out. Jesus on the other hand, reminded people of the heart of God, treasures on earth is a proving ground of stewardship, you do not get to keep, but trade it to God for a greater reward. *'Lay not up for yourselves treasures upon earth, where moth and rust does corrupt, and where thieves break through and steal: But lay up for yourselves treasures in heaven, where neither moth nor rust does corrupt, and where thieves do not break through nor steal:*

For where your treasure is, there will your heart be also."(Mathew 6:19-21)

Those who come to God last, are to be treated as a child coming into a natural family. When my third daughter was born, my two older daughters were so excited when we brought baby girl home. They loved on her, celebrated her and besides all of that, they began to serve her. Was willing to do any and everything to ensure she was in want for nothing. This is the depiction of Heaven and the kingdom. We should serve those who come to the church last, as if they were new born babies, because in the kingdom, no matter the age, when you give your life to God, you are born again…a new born.

Whether my girls knew it or not, when their baby sister came home and they first laid eyes on her, love caused, *"The first to become last, and last became first."*

*So what the church originally was established on; love, miracles, signs and wonders, will happen in the last days. **This church has been made last**, but God will make her first again. **The true church** was built on things money could not buy. This is the reason the religious leaders were determined to destroy Jesus and his movement…the church, it showed too much of CHRIST AND HIS POWER. Jesus himself will Resurrect the church from the ashes. **The church says….come Lord Jesus…***

*"Jesus replied, "Blessed are you, Simon son of Jonah, for this was not revealed to you by flesh and blood, but by my Father in heaven. And I tell you that you are Peter, **and upon this rock I will build my Church, and the gates of Hell will not overcome it.** I will give you the keys of the kingdom of heaven; whatever you bind on earth will be bound in heaven, and whatever you loose on earth will be loosed in heaven."" (Matthew 16:17-19 NIV)*

CHAPTER ELEVEN
The G.O.A.T.

Who is the GOAT?

What is the nature of the GOAT? I know it's popular in our present and pop culture as accomplished and great, but what is it? Where did this come from? This praise and worship?

We are so quick to follow the world, but, God is the leader and creator of all living things. What is He saying about the greatest? You have to watch this devil He's on a mission to set up his throne in the earth. He wants to be God so bad…it hurts.

The Goat is the spirit of Anti-Christ. He is on his way. Everything God is, this counterfeit wants it! Beware people of God, decree and declare. Watch what you say out of your mouth. Your words carry power. **When you see Jesus, trust and believe, you won't want to be somebody's GOAT! Not at ALL!**

So tell me, if Jesus was preaching a powerful message, as always, would his disciples yell out, " Jesus the GOAT? You're a GOAT Jesus!" What do you think Jesus would say or do?

We should want to be just like Him. I heard someone call a bishop "GOAT"..and it shot through me! Keep that one to yourself...don't ever call God's people goats. We sing "Lamb of God" then call each other goat (curse). Don't you know about the "scape goat, " it carried the curse of one's sin and was driven into the wilderness?

* * *

Stand up church. It's a violation of your Kingdom Rights to be called out of your name by one of your own. Rebuked in love to save , even if you think you don't need saving.

Well, Lucifer is the original GOAT! He rebelled and his children are rebellious! The disobedient one! We are living in a time of rebellion. I am not politically correct, we have enough of those. The kingdom of God is RIGHTEOUSNESS...not political!   We need to turn back to God, but in order to do that, we must first know our position and our place, in Him. We get caught up in trends and fads, but God is the same, he never changes.

The apostles were so serious about God's church...they took a stand for Righteousness. How disrespectful it is for any Man of God or Woman of God to be called a GOAT. I listen, honor and respect the people of God, gifts, talents and their achievements,   but wait a minute! GOAT?   Jesus makes some things crystal clear and I listen to Him above all. Listen to what our Lord had to say about this;

"When the Son of Man comes in his glory, and all the angels with him, he will sit on his glorious throne. All the nations will be gathered before him, and he will separate the people one from another as a shepherd separates the sheep from the goats. He will put the sheep on his right and the goats on his left.

"Then the King will say to those on his right, 'Come, you who are blessed by my Father; take your inheritance, the kingdom prepared for you since the creation of the world. For I was hungry and you gave me something to eat, I was thirsty and you gave me something to drink, I was a stranger and you invited me in, I needed clothes and you clothed me, I was sick and you looked after me, I was in prison and you came to visit me.' "Then the righteous will answer him, 'Lord, when did we see you hungry and feed you, or thirsty and give you something to drink?

When did we see you sick or in prison and go to visit you?' "The King will reply, 'Truly I tell you, whatever you did for one of the least of these brothers and sisters of mine, you did for me.' "Then he will say to those on his left, 'Depart from me, you who are cursed, into the eternal fire prepared for the devil and his angels. I was a stranger and you did not invite me in, I needed clothes and you did not clothe me, I was sick and in prison and you did not look after me.'

"They also will answer, 'Lord, when did we see you hungry or thirsty or a stranger or needing clothes or sick or in prison, and did not help you?' "He will reply, 'Truly I tell you, whatever you did not do for one of the least of these, you did not do for me.' "Then they will go away to eternal punishment, but the righteous to eternal life." (Matthew 25:31-37, 39-41, 43-46)NIV

Then I saw in the right hand of him who sat on the throne a scroll with writing on both sides and sealed with seven seals. And I saw a mighty angel proclaiming in a loud voice, "Who is worthy to break the seals and open the scroll?"

But no one in heaven or on earth or under the earth could open the scroll or even look inside it. I wept and wept because no one was found who was worthy to open the scroll or look inside. Then I saw a Lamb, looking as if it had been slain, standing at the center of the throne, encircled by the four living creatures and the elders.

The Lamb had seven horns and seven eyes, which are the seven spirits of God sent out into all the earth. He went and took the scroll from the right hand of him who sat on the throne. And when he had taken it, the four living creatures and the twenty-four elders fell down before the Lamb. Each one had a harp and they were holding golden bowls full of incense, which are the prayers of God's people.

And they sang a new song, saying: "You are worthy to take the scroll and to open its seals, because you were slain, and with your blood you purchased for God persons from every tribe and language and people and nation. You have made them to be a kingdom and priests to serve our God, and they will reign on the earth."

Then I looked and heard the voice of many angels, numbering thousands upon thousands, and ten thousand times ten thousand. They encircled the throne and the living creatures and the elders. In a loud voice they were saying: "Worthy is the Lamb, who was slain, to receive power and wealth and wisdom and strength and honor and glory and praise!"

Then I heard every creature in heaven and on earth and under the

earth and on the sea, and all that is in them, saying: "To him who sits on the throne and to the Lamb be praise and honor and glory and power, for ever and ever!" The four living creatures said, "Amen," and the elders fell down and worshiped.
   (Revelation 5:1-4, 6-14)

We may play these games while we are on earth, but when we are in His presence, we will know that God is nothing to play with. So many people wish they could come back for a second chance, and are forbidden and restricted. Life is after death and we will give an account for our life here. Don't let the videos fool you...

I rest my case and if I were you, I wouldn't play both sides. "You can't serve two masters, you will hate the one or love the other."

To the left buddy!

Lucifer know's who the "Greatest Of All Times" is and it's definitely, not him!

CHAPTER TWELVE

The Antidote

It all started in the garden with a serpent (snake) deceiving Eve at the tree. Then we have the account of the children of Israel being delivered from slavery, by the hand of Pharaoh of Egypt. They were oppressed and abused for over 400 years. When the time came for them to be delivered , they went into the wilderness, where they did many things to anger God.

Brasen Serpent (Bronze Snake)

"They traveled from Mount Hor along the route to the Red Sea, to go around Edom. But the people grew impatient on the way; they spoke against God and against Moses, and said, "Why have you brought us up out of Egypt to die in the wilderness? There is no bread! There is no water! And we detest this miserable food!" Then the Lord sent venomous snakes among them; they bit the people and many Israelites died. The people came to Moses and said, "We sinned when we spoke against the Lord and against you. Pray that the Lord will take the snakes away from us." So Moses prayed for the people. The Lord said to Moses, "Make a snake and put it up on a pole; anyone who is bitten can look at it and live." So Moses made a bronze snake and put it up on a pole. Then when anyone was bitten by a snake and looked at the bronze snake, they lived."

Numbers 21:4-9 NIV

"Just as Moses lifted up the snake in the wilderness, so the Son of Man must be lifted up, that everyone who believes may have eternal life in him."

John 3:14-15 NIV

* * *

Jesus came down through 42 generations to get to Calvary's Cross. Jesus knew his purpose and what he had to do. This serpent killed all of the prophets along the way. Jesus called the religious leaders, prude vipers. All of those generations, Jesus with Father was collecting all this samples for venom, and blood for the "Antidote" in which he was the last and final part to complete the cure. They needed all of the samples of blood, along with uncontaminated blood to produce the antibodies.

All of the prophets and righteous form Abel to Jesus was collecting data of all of the poisonous snakes in this earth. This thing is spiritual. We can see things in the natural, to compare to the spiritual. The righteous are like the scientist risking their lives seeking to find a cure to save so many others.

""*Woe to you, teachers of the law and Pharisees, you hypocrites! You build tombs for the prophets and decorate the graves of the righteous. And you say, 'If we had lived in the days of our ancestors, we would not have taken part with them in shedding **the blood of the prophets.**' So you testify against yourselves that you are the descendants of those who murdered the prophets.*

Go ahead, then, and complete what your ancestors started! **"You Snakes!** *You brood of vipers! How will you escape being condemned to hell? Therefore I am sending you prophets and sages and teachers. Some of them you will kill and crucify; others you will flog in your synagogues and pursue from town to town.* **And so upon you will come all the righteous blood that has been shed on earth, from the blood of righteous Abel to the blood of Zechariah son of Berekiah, whom you murdered between the temple and the altar.**

Truly I tell you, all this will come on this generation. "Jerusalem, Jerusalem, you who kill the prophets and stone those sent to you, how often I have longed to gather your children together, as a hen gathers her chicks under her wings, and you were not willing. Look, your house is left to you desolate. For I tell you, you will not see me again until you say, 'Blessed is he who comes in the name of the Lord.'"
Matthew 23:29-39 NIV

Remember when Jesus was born? Why would the son of God be born around animals rather than in his own house...His Father's House the temple?

Reason being, these same vipers and snakes he's talking to are the very snakes who were running the temple despised as priests and holy men. They would have immediately turned him over to king Herod who was looking for Jesus as a bay king to kill him He went to the temple to test them at the age of 12 and they din't see him again in that form until he was 30 years of age.

"After Jesus was born in Bethlehem in Judea, during the time of King Herod, Magi from the east came to Jerusalem and asked, "Where is the one who has been born king of the Jews? We saw his star when it rose and have come to worship him." When King Herod heard this he was disturbed, and all Jerusalem with him.

*When he had called together all the people's **chief priests and teachers of the law,** he asked them where the Messiah was to be born. "In Bethlehem in Judea," they replied, "for this is what the prophet has written: " 'But you, Bethlehem, in the land of Judah, are by no means least among the rulers of Judah; for out of you will come a ruler who will shepherd my people Israel.'"*

Then Herod called the Magi secretly and found out from them the exact time the star had appeared. After they had heard the king, they went on their way, and the star they had seen when it rose went ahead of them until it stopped over the place where the child was. When they saw the star, they were overjoyed. On coming to the house, they saw the child with his mother Mary, and they bowed down and worshiped him. Then they opened their treasures and presented him with gifts of gold, frankincense and myrrh.

*And having been warned in a dream not to go back to Herod, they returned to their country by another route. When they had gone, an angel of the Lord appeared to Joseph in a dream. "Get up," he said, "take the child and his mother and escape to Egypt. **Stay there until I tell you, for Herod is going to search for the child to kill him."** So he got up, took the child and his mother during the night and left for Egypt, where he stayed until the death of Herod.*

*And so was fulfilled what the Lord had said through the prophet: "**Out of Egypt I called my son."** When Herod realized that he had been outwitted by the Magi, he was furious, and he gave orders to kill all the boys in Bethlehem and its vicinity who were two years old and under, in accordance with the time he had learned from the Magi. Then what was said through the prophet Jeremiah was fulfilled: "*

* * *

A voice is heard in Ramah, weeping and great mourning, Rachel weeping for her children and refusing to be comforted, because they are no more." After Herod died, an angel of the Lord appeared in a dream to Joseph in Egypt and said, "Get up, take the child and his mother and go to the land of Israel, for those who were trying to take the child's life are dead."

So he got up, took the child and his mother and went to the land of Israel. But when he heard that Archelaus was reigning in Judea in place of his father Herod, he was afraid to go there. Having been warned in a dream, he withdrew to the district of Galilee, and he went and lived in a town called Nazareth. So was fulfilled what was said through the prophets, that he would be called a Nazarene."
   Matthew 2:1-7, 9-23 NIV

Do you see how Jesus was calling them snakes? Think about the science behind seeking cures and antidotes. Think about all of the lives that were lost doing research? How many scientists and explorers were bitten and died, but got a little closer to find a cure? Jesus came down through forty-two generations, *"Thus there were fourteen generations in all from Abraham to David, fourteen from David to the exile to Babylon, and fourteen from the exile to the Messiah." Matthew 1:17 NIV*
Jesus came to fulfill the Law, not to destroy. He needed the Law and The Prophets, for his victory defeat of this snake and his offspring, who has been taking lives since the days of Adam and Eve.

We see in the natural but this thing is spiritual, "You are Israel's teacher," said Jesus, "and do you not understand these things? I have spoken to you of earthly things and you do not believe; how then will you believe if I speak of heavenly things? No one has ever gone into heaven except the one who came from heaven—the Son of Man. Just as Moses lifted up the snake in the wilderness, so the Son of Man must be lifted up, that everyone who believes may have eternal life in him."
   John 3:10, 12-15 NIV
Jesus brutal death represents, the attack of every venomous snake, he was bitten constantly and violently. All the poison of these vipers he took and didn't open his mouth. He took the pain and pressure of the jaws releasing the venom, of that SERPENT and his seed.

* * *

After Jesus was raised up, the process began. Remember when John called Jesus, the Lamb of God who came to wash away the sins of the world.

Scientist use antibodies of lambs, sheep, goats and horses to name a few. Jesus embodied the full process of obtaining the cure for mankind, not only to be reconciled back to God, but to be totally restored and made priest and kings. God gave us back our authority. A lamb without sin…pure blood, His blood mixed with the venom of the serpent and our sins.

Moses, Elijah and Jesus are the only men recorded in the Bible who went into the wilderness and fasted forty days and nights without food. Many thought Moses had died when he went up on Sinai to meet with God. They didn't think a human could survive that long at that altitude. Moses came back with the law. When Moses disobeyed God and hit the rock (out of anger against the people) rather than speaking to it, to get water, for the people. For this reason, God told him he would not crossover to the Promise Land after leading the children of Israel for forty long years. God allowed Moses to see the land for the mountain and called him to come up and be with God to die.

The prophet Elijah was caught up in a chariot and was translated not see death, naturally, (Elijah was sent back to life as John the Baptist).

"But I tell you, Elijah has come, and they have done to him everything they wished, just as it is written about him.""Mark 9:13 NIV

Jesus held a meeting with Moses and Elijah on a high Mountain where he was transfigured, right before three witness eyes besides Jesus, Moses and Elijah. What did Moses and the Prophet Elijah possess, that Jesus needed. These three were at work on the plan of salvation. This happened shortly before Jesus was to be put to death by the Pharisees.

"And he said to them, "Truly I tell you, some who are standing here will not taste death before they see that the kingdom of God has come with power."

After six days Jesus took Peter, James and John with him and led them up a high mountain, where they were all alone. There he was transfigured before them. His clothes became dazzling white, whiter than anyone in the world could bleach them. And there appeared before them Elijah and Moses, who were talking with Jesus.

Peter said to Jesus, "Rabbi, it is good for us to be here. Let us put up three shelters—one for you, one for Moses and one for Elijah." (He did not know what to say, they were so frightened.) Then a cloud appeared and covered them, and a voice came from the cloud: "This is my Son, whom I love. Listen to him!" Suddenly, when they looked around, they no longer saw anyone with them except Jesus.

As they were coming down the mountain, Jesus gave them orders not to tell anyone what they had seen until the Son of Man had risen from the dead. And they asked him, "Why do the teachers of the law say that Elijah must come first?" Jesus replied, "To be sure, Elijah does come first, and restores all things. Why then is it written that the Son of Man must suffer much and be rejected? But I tell you, Elijah has come, and they have done to him everything they wished, just as it is written about him.""Mark 9:1-9, 11-13 NIV

*The suffering of these people of the past were those who were willing to lay down their lives for the cause. As great scientist who are determined to find a cure, to save thousand…millions. They went into areas of live no one had gone before and died, seeking to make an eternal difference. **Jesus blood represents the last and final antibodies need for the cure to sin. Jesus blood is our "Antidote," and just like the scientific facts below, people are dying a senseless deaths because they won't come to Jesus and his agents for the antidote for Satan's snake bite to humanity.***

This is why Jesus said, to them,"Go into all the world and preach the gospel to all creation. And these signs will accompany those who believe: In my name they will drive out demons; they will speak in new tongues; they will pick up snakes with their hands; and when they drink deadly poison, it will not hurt them at all; they will place their hands on sick people, and they will get well."

After the Lord Jesus had spoken to them, he was taken up into heaven and he sat at the right hand of God. Then the disciples went out and preached everywhere, and the Lord worked with them and confirmed his word by the signs that accompanied it."Mark 16:15, 17-20 NIV

* * *

145

It took the holy blood of Jesus who knew no sin, mixed with the venom of the serpent (Satan) to make the antidote which is the cure for our sins. After the right formula, Jesus had to take it to his Father in heaven, to get His approval and endorsement.

Remember what he said to Mary after he resurrected, "Touch me not, because I haven't yet ascended to my Father." This is the evidence that Jesus went down into hell first, defeated death, hell and the grave, then across the gulf, he went to paradise to set free those who were believers who died by faith under the Law of Moses and the prophets. All through the scriptures you hear the coming of the Messiah. They understood they couldn't go to heaven until the Messiah came.

Remember Adam and Eve in the Garden of Eden? They would wait for God to come to visit them everyday. They could not go to heaven to visit God, they only could see Him when He came to them. Same principle for these of the Old Testament or Torah.,so, Paradise was hidden in the earth (beneath the earth). When Jesus got the victory beneath the earth, he took the keys from the enemy. All of those waiting on him as the righteous of the Lord according to the Law, were set free.

"…And He set the captives free." They left

 So for the first time, those of the past were granted access to heaven.

This is Spiritual and eternal, what the Lord has done for all of us, if we just believe and receive the ANTIDOTE of Salvation…Jesus is the Only cure…He truly paid the price to save us!

Snakebites kill up to 94,000 people worldwide every year, with the highest number of deaths in South Asia and sub-Saharan Africa.

The main obstacle to saving lives is the global availability of anti-venom. Until fairly recently, the gold standard has been a targeted anti-venom that works against a specific species of snake. But that means doctors must know exactly which snake out of around 600 possible species did the deed, and that makes individual anti-venom costly to stock.

* * *

In Africa, the most effective treatment has been a multipurpose anti-venom that works against a variety of vipers and cobras found on the continent. But according to current reports, stockpiles of this anti-venom are expected to run out in June 2016. The main supplier, a French pharmaceutical company, halted production because the anti-venom was no longer profitable.

Now, scientists in Thailand have found a way to make a single anti-venom that works against 18 species of snake found in Asia and Africa. The team maintains that their version will be more affordable and more widely useful, helping to bring anti-venom to the resource-strapped regions that need it most.

Currently, the only known treatment is anti-venom; an approach implemented in 1896 by Albert Calmette based on antibodies collected from horses and sheep that have become immune to the toxins in the venom. Although this treatment has saved many lives, it is weakly effective as snake venoms and their toxins vary significantly across all subspecies and only 10 to 15 per cent of the antibodies in the sera bind to the venom. To effect cure, multiple vials of anti-venom are often needed but each additional vial induces higher levels of adverse side effects and increased treatment costs. (Source: University of Bristol)

After all the sacrifices, hard work and lives lost, to develop a cure, saving lives always was and is the goal. Why aren't more people taking the shot, protecting themselves and their love ones, and getting cured? keep it with you wherever you go, just in case you ever get bitten again...

Then Jesus said to them, "I have given you authority to trample on snakes and scorpions and to overcome all the power of the enemy; nothing will harm you."
   Luke 10:19 NIV

5 HOLES

The Pharisees (religious leaders) constantly asked Jesus to do miracles for them and prove who he was? Jesus never performed for the Pharisees, neither showed them miracles. What he left on record for his followers is this, never try to show who you are to those who are blinded by the their sins and religion, always fighting for traditions, rather than good of the people. The Pharisees were very educated and knowledgeable about God, but couldn't recognize Him when He was right in their faces. They called the God they claimed to serve and love, "a Devil!"

When Jesus Resurrected from the dead, he was raise with a new glorified body. This baby was like flesh but has the ability do what spirit can do. He talked with them (his disciples), ate food and drank with them. Remember when He walked through the wall and said to Thomas, "put your hands into the holes in my hands and feet, thrust your hands into my side?"

"My Lord and My God!" Said Thomas.

Why would Jesus construct a new glorified body, but keep FIVE holes from the old body?

- 1 Evidence, and witnesses against his enemies on Judgement Day

- 2 It's a reminder to heaven and hell how God's enemies gave it their best shot and as much pain as was when they did it, it doesn't hurt anymore

- 3 It didn't stop anything, especially God's love, the hate empowered Him, because they thought they took His life, but the truth is, He laid down His life and didn't fight.

- 4 He asked God to forgive them, even when He was in His worst pain. They didn't make Him bitter or unforgiving. He came back as if they did nothing to Him.

- Five, His Church was birthed out of those bloody holes. Five is the number of grace. The Church of the New Testament was birth out of Grace, the Old Church was birthed from the Law. The Law was used to kill Jesus, while Grace was there to Raise Him up!

"Wherefore he saith, When he ascended up on high, he led captivity captive,

And gave gifts unto men. (Now that he ascended, what is it but that he also descended first into the lower parts of the earth? He that descended is the same also that ascended up far above all heavens, that he might fill all things.)"

And he gave some, apostles; and some, prophets; and some, evangelists; and some, pastors and teachers; *for the perfecting of the saints, for the work of the ministry, for the edifying of the body of Christ: till we all come in the unity of the faith, and of the knowledge of the Son of God, unto a perfect man, unto the measure of the stature of the fulness of Christ:*

That we henceforth be no more children, tossed to and fro, and carried about with every wind of doctrine, by the sleight of men, and cunning craftiness, whereby they lie in wait to deceive; but speaking the truth in love, may grow up into him in all things, which is the head, even Christ:

From whom the whole body fitly joined together and compacted by that which every joint supplies, according to the effectual working in the measure of every part, makes increase of the body unto the edifying of itself in love." Ephesians 4:8-16 KJV

Who gave, and who ascended up far above all heavens? JESUS! NOBODY BUT JESUS!

Don't let these modern day Pharisees tell you there are no more apostles and prophets. As long as Jesus is alive and we are in this earth with His Holy Spirit, there will be **Fivefold Ministry!** Bid will continue to reveal himself to His children, not Satan's children. Didn't you hear when Jesus called the religious leaders, the devil's children?

These false teachers want to make you believe there is no more fivefold ministry, so they can be your twofold ministry, "Lucifer and Satan" as your teachers, and they will definitely do it straight from the Bible, (remember how many scriptures Satan quoted to Jesus in the wilderness) by twisting words and always tearing down people who are trying to make a difference in peoples's lives…for the better.

Information will never supersede *REVELATION!* Jesus gave the devil back God's word, but with REVELATION! This is why Jesus gave and revealed to the apostle John, *the Book of Revelation,* and not the book of just…*information.*

* * *

The Pharisees were a very, highly educated and knowledgeable group, but they had zero revelation. You can study and read about God all of your life, but never meet Him or know Him? Studying you can get some good information, but on the other side of that, spending time with God will cause Him to reveal Himself to you…that's REVELATION!

Those Five Holes in Jesus body right still till this day, represents the relationship and blood covenant between Him and His Church, and those in whom, He has chosen to feed His sheep (people).

If you are called to the ministry, you are the power of those holes in Jesus body, and He will never leave you alone, because when He kept those holes in His body, He kept you in His HEART.

They will hate you, just as much as they hated Jesus. Don't be fooled by them knowing scriptures and the word, the Pharisees did the same, beware of false teachers coming in Jesus name. They make a living off of you claiming to be exposing other false prophets and giving you supposedly sound doctrine. Listen closely, they preach hate, envy and jealousy more than anything. They talk about other preachers more than they talk about Jesus.

The great commission given to us by our Lord Jesus is' "Go into all the world and preach this gospel (good news) of the kingdom."

We as followers of Jesus Christ are called to love and Satan' followers are demonstrators of hate. Listen closely to whom ever you're following and you'll know according to the teachings of Jesus who they truly are working for?

Never forget this while doing ministry, Jesus death was a HATE CRIME!

What kingdom are you really working for and who are you truly representing?

"And Jesus came and spake unto them, saying, All power is given unto me in heaven and in earth. Go ye therefore, and teach all nations, baptizing them in the name of the Father, and of the Son, and of the Holy Ghost: teaching them to observe all things whatsoever I have commanded you: and, lo, I am with you alway, even unto the end of the world. Amen."Matthew 28:18-20 KJV

Jesus gave God his best offering and worship. He sacrificed his life, Nobody took his life, he laid it down. Jesus is alive and well, why would He not talk to His people, who are contending with the enemy everyday because of who He is to us and who we are to Him? When God's children want to talk to Him, they will, and when the Father wants to talk to His children, then He can, and He will!

False teachers want you to believe that God only talks through His word written, so foolish. I'm inspired to write this book by Jesus Christ, the author and finisher of my faith.

As the author, if someone reads this book and wanted to talk to me as the author and I agreed to talk with them, how would it make any kind of since, if someone else who read my book, but never, have met me or had access to me, tell you, (who have met me, and talked to me) that you only can know the author by what's written in his book? That is RIDICULOUS!

 If I am alive and well, and willing to talk with you personally? You, can get a lot more, if we have a relationship. Don't substitute your relationship with God, for a counterfeit.

Think about this, A stranger who have read your father's book, is teaching your father's very own children about their father, because he has read one of your father's book. Then tell you, any attempt you make to contact your father is impossible, because he only talks through one book. Everything you will ever know about your father, is in that one book. Do you really believe that God is done? That this generation doesn't have anything to offer God, that would be worthy of writing in books, leaving a record of testimonials for generations to come?

Listen, the Lord wants you!
God is not dead! When Peter and the others went to do ministry, they did not take scrolls with them (books) they were not allowed to

touch God's written word. So, understanding what Jesus had told them in the 3 1/2 years of teaching and ministry, they became the Living Word of God. Then they became so effective, they were writing more books, like the Book of Acts for example.

Listen! Establish a personal relationship with your Heavenly Father, continue to read and study, but let nothing take the place of spending quality time with your Daddy. Get rid of the blockers, who may have mastered the book, but not a person relationship with The Lord Jesus Christ.

People are dying senseless deaths spiritually, because of Satan's bites(lies and deception). For the same exact reasons as to those who are dying in some of our earthly regions.

Dying unnecessary deaths, because of these poisonous snakes, simply, because they don't have access or refuse take the **"Antidote."**

Jesus said this before He was crucified, " Just as Moses lifted up the serpent in the wilderness, so must the son of man be lived up, and If I am lifted up, I will draw all men unto me."

ANTIDOTE!

CHAPTER THIRTEEN

Benediction

The Resurrection of Christ

"Now, brothers and sisters, I want to remind you of the gospel I preached to you, which you received and on which you have taken your stand. By this gospel you are saved, if you hold firmly to the word I preached to you. Otherwise, you have believed in vain.

For what I received I passed on to you as of first importance: that Christ died for our sins according to the Scriptures, that he was buried, that he was raised on the third day according to the Scriptures, and that he appeared to Cephas, and then to the Twelve.

After that, he appeared to more than five hundred of the brothers and sisters at the same time, most of whom are still living, though some have fallen asleep. Then he appeared to James, then to all the apostles, and last of all he appeared to me also, as to one abnormally born (being Paul was not of the original Twelve disciples hand picked by Jesus while on earth. Saul who later becomes Paul by conversion, had the privilege of seeing Jesus up in the heavens. When Jesus showed Himself to him and called Saul/Paul to the ministry, he was struck with blindness, lost his natural sight, and in exchanged, received 20/20 vision and revelations in the realm of the spirit.. Fact, Saul was on his way to persecute and kill the church, stop the (movement!) *For I am the least of the apostles and do not even deserve to be called an apostle, because I persecuted the church of God.*

* * *

But by the grace of God I am what I am, and his grace to me was not without effect. No, I worked harder than all of them—yet not I, but the grace of God that was with me. Whether, then, it is I or they, this is what we preach, and this is what you believed."
1 Corinthians 15:1-11 NIV

The Resurrection of the Dead

"But if it is preached that Christ has been raised from the dead, how can some of you say that there is no resurrection of the dead? If there is no resurrection of the dead, then not even Christ has been raised. And if Christ has not been raised, our preaching is useless and so is your faith. More than that, we are then found to be false witnesses about God, for we have testified about God that he raised Christ from the dead. But he did not raise him if in fact the dead are not raised. For if the dead are not raised, then Christ has not been raised either.

And if Christ has not been raised, your faith is futile; you are still in your sins. Then those also who have fallen asleep in Christ are lost. If only for this life we have hope in Christ, we are of all people most to be pitied. But Christ has indeed been raised from the dead, the first fruits of those who have fallen asleep. For since death came through a man, the resurrection of the dead comes also through a man. For as in Adam all die, so in Christ all will be made alive."
1 Corinthians 15:12-22 NIV
https://bible.com/bible/111/1co.15.12-22.NIV

The Resurrection Body

"But someone will ask, "How are the dead raised? With what kind of body will they come?" How foolish! What you sow does not come to life unless it dies. When you sow, you do not plant the body that will be, but just a seed, perhaps of wheat or of something else.

But God gives it a body as he has determined, and to each kind of seed he gives its own body. Not all flesh is the same: People have one kind of flesh, animals have another, birds another and fish another. There are also heavenly bodies and there are earthly bodies; but the splendor of the heavenly bodies is one kind, and the splendor of the earthly bodies is another.

The sun has one kind of splendor, the moon another and the stars another; and star differs from star in splendor. So will it be with the resurrection of the dead. The body that is sown is perishable, it is raised imperishable; it is sown in dishonor, it is raised in glory; it is sown in weakness, it is raised in power; it is sown a natural body, it is raised a spiritual body. If there is a natural body, there is also a spiritual body. So it is written: "The first man Adam became a living being"; the last Adam, a life-giving spirit.

The spiritual did not come first, but the natural, and after that the spiritual. The first man was of the dust of the earth; the second man is of heaven. As was the earthly man, so are those who are of the earth; and as is the heavenly man, so also are those who are of heaven. And just as we have borne the image of the earthly man, so shall we bear the image of the heavenly man. I declare to you, brothers and sisters, that flesh and blood cannot inherit the kingdom of God, nor does the perishable inherit the imperishable.

Listen, I tell you a mystery: We will not all sleep, but we will all be changed— in a flash, in the twinkling of an eye, at the last trumpet. For the trumpet will sound, the dead will be raised imperishable, and we will be changed. For the perishable must clothe itself with the imperishable, and the mortal with immortality. When the perishable has been clothed with the imperishable, and the mortal with immortality, then the saying that is written will come true: "Death has been swallowed up in victory." "Where, O death, is your victory? Where, O death, is your sting?"

The sting of death is sin, and the power of sin is the law. But thanks be to God! He gives us the victory through our Lord Jesus Christ. Therefore, my dear brothers and sisters, stand firm. Let nothing move you. Always give yourselves fully to the work of the Lord, because you know that your labor in the Lord is not in vain."
1 Corinthians 15:35-58 NIV
https://bible.com/bible/111/1co.15.35-58.NIV

We need to understand when we read the writings of the apostles and prophets, they under the Law of Moses. So death is called "Sleep." When one died, they went to the underworld, Whether Paradise or Hell. Hades as many call it, was a shared space with Paradise. When the rich man and Lazarus died, they could see each other, although they were not permitted to be in the same space and feel the same things. https://luke.bible/luke-16-23

So is death not knowing or none existing? No…death is, separation from God, who is good, and all of the good things that comes, with and from that relationship. Listen to the conversation they were having in the underworld. The people who died according to faith in the Law or lived their life by the light which was in their hearts, went to Paradise. On the other hand, those who were considered evil and wicked, went to the other side of Paradise, (hell) waiting for the Messiah as well, they had no rest and it wasn't comfortable. For judgment…maybe not now, or right away? But nonetheless, they would be hoping for mercy, because now they know without a doubt, there is, "Life After Death" or "Life After Life."

They were waiting by faith, on the Messiah and the Day of Judgment. This is why Mary said, to Jesus, " I know my brother will rise on that DAY." Jesus was there to show them of what all the generations were waiting on, since the beginning of time. Now, it was finally here! "I AM the RESURRECTION", Jesus said. Amazingly, what they had been waiting on for so long was right there in their presence, but they didn't recognize Him, because it didn't look like, what most imagined. How many times has God answered your prayers and the answer looks nothing like what you'd imagined?

At the tomb of Lazarus along with his sisters, family and friends, "Jesus wept." Why would Jesus be weeping? We know He loved Lazarus, or should I say, loves,"him. We know it could not be because of Lazarus' Death, Jesus knew he would be "sleep" as He called it, to his disciples. He could have just sent His word to heal him. Jesus did not have to be physically there. Jesus wept because of the presence of all those religious leaders (Pharisees and Sadducees) who have been preaching and teaching for so long about the Messiah to the people, but soon after this Lazarus' resurrection, that they would condemn Him, find fault in Him and even lie on Him to get rid of Him. These were direct decedents of Abraham and Moses, and Jesus loved them both for many reasons, and Abraham and Moses loved Him. John 8:12-49, 51-59 KJV

https://bible.com/bible/1/jhn.8.58-59.KJV

"I am the God of Abraham, and the God of Isaac, and the God of Jacob? God is not the God of the dead, but of the living."
Matthew 22:32 KJV

Jesus cried, because He knew those who were considered preaches and priests, great men of God, would set him up, lie on him, turn him over to the Romans, and they hated the Romans, but not enough to protect their own. These were considered the most holy of men. These men even after seeing and witnessing the miracle of life come into a man after four days in the grave, they were right there when Jesus raised Lazarus from the dead. He knew Moses and Abraham would see children of theirs cast down to hell. Jesus knew whatever he did, it would never be enough. As much as I love Abraham and Moss, their children were of the devil.

So here is the long awaited Messiah and they didn't even recognize Him. He was even at the grave of Lazarus, to raise him from the underworld. I believe Lazarus was there with Father Abraham, Moses, David and the prophets, just everybody, who all were waiting on the Messiah, to get them from, beneath the earth. Especially, this divided place with a Gulf between them. Although the righteous were not actually being tormented themselves, it had to be somewhat challenging, to hear and see people suffering, no matter what they did to you in the earth, and or in their lifetime…this is not what true followers of Christ desire.

When Jesus said to the one the thieves, "Today you will be with me in paradise." Take note, He didn't say in Heaven. Reason being, their's no place of torment in heaven. Secondly, all of the prophecies point to the victory of the coming Messiah, so destiny put Him in war. Jesus had to get the victory and He did win, against, death, hell and the grave."

When Jesus resurrected, He set the captives free (all of those died (slept) waiting on the coming of the Messiah. When Jesus set all those from the past world free, they came up and on earth.

"Jesus, when he had cried again with a loud voice, yielded up the ghost. and

the graves were opened; and many bodies of the saints which slept arose, and came out of the graves after his resurrection, and went into the holy city, and appeared unto many.

Now when the centurion, and they that were with him, watching Jesus, saw the earthquake, and those things that were done, they feared greatly, saying, Truly this was the Son of God. And many women were there beholding afar off, which followed Jesus from Galilee, ministering unto him: among which was Mary Magdalene, and Mary the mother of James and Joses, and the mother of Zebedee's children."
Matthew 27:50, 52-56 KJV
https://bible.com/bible/1/mat.27.50-56.KJV

When Jesus set the peoples of the past free from the underworld, he left a big ole empty space in that place. Now there were not anyone who died by faith believing that the Messiah was coming one day to set them free. Remember how God would visit Adam, but Adam could not go to visit God. Two different bodies, of two different dimensions. Now what FREE is and or means; Now we love with the Father in Heaven. No more visits, no more wondering or waiting! When you take your last breath in time, you take your first light in Heaven. No sleeping, no resting, no underworld for the righteous, we go home! IMMEDIATELY! All of the sleep references are before the RESURRECTION!

As we read the letters from the apostles, it took them a minute to get it, but they did get it! Understand they were still transitioning from the Law to Grace. "To be absent of the body, is to be present with the Lord."

RIP…REST IN PEACE OR RIP…RESURRECT IN POWER?

When Jesus was Resurrected Himself and was outside of the tomb where they had laid Him, remember what He said to Mary, "Touch me not, because I have not yet ascended to the Father." Jesus is letting us know right there, that He was in the underworld taking care of business in eternity and got it done with a body… a spiritual body. Whenever anything has to do with spirits, we make it spooky and eerie, when the truth of the matter is, we all are a spirit. Those who operate in, the earthly realm are illegal residents, if they have no physical body. Jesus was taking the Father all He had done and collected, that would ultimately save all of us who want to be save, because Jesus paid the price.

Look at how powerful the RESURRECTION was at that time, and look at how many women believed and had no fear for their lives. No matter what we do, there are no leaving women out of History. They were bold and fearless! Jesus chose them to be His first witnesses of the flesh, to see Him model His new glorified body.

Living in a physical body on earth, but gain a spiritual body when we are called to leave this world.

Even today, many of us were made to believe that *The Resurrection* was a much anticipated event. But it is a "person, a real person" in the person of our, Lord and Savior Jesus Christ.

When I was trying to explain how I got up out go my sleep, walked the floor, then start to elevate with no say or control, I was ascended into the heavens. When I arrived, I sat and I hate and I had feelings, and awareness, but no hurt or pains, physical or mental. It just felt good! My testimony is true, and I don't struggle with resting, dying or any other thing, outside of God's Word and His witnesses. If you haven't experienced something, then, it's education or information.

Jesus said for us to be, "WITNESSES!"

THAT'S REVELATION!

LOVE...LOVE...LOVE

After all of this, I wouldn't want to end this book without giving you an opportunity to know Jesus as your Lord and Savior , if you have not been formally introduced to Him or been invited? If you don't know Him, I am sure you can find Him after reading, "RESURRECTION."

First of all, God loves you, He died for you. God loves the "Backslider" and He misses you. No matter what you have done or doing, we want you back at home. As your brother in the Kingdom and of Christ, I'm welcoming you back home. I know it's hard, especially, when you know why you left in the first place. But all things considered, you don't belong out there. Come home! I feel you in my spirit, I'm in tears as I write this to you. Come back home.

We can start by, just saying this simple prayer with me;
Lord Jesus, I'm a sinner. I believe you died for me and my sins, and I am a sinner. I believe you love that much. I believe that only you can save me. Forgive me. I need you. I want to be saved, I want to become a new person and live a new life through You. Lord, I denounce everything that's not like you. Jesus I choose you. I give my life to you from this day forward. Even when I makes mistakes, I still belong to you and I am never leaving you, because you promised, never to leave me. Teach me your ways oh Lord. I make you Lord over my life and all that I have and all that I am.
Thank you Jesus for saving me!
Now praise God for welcoming you into the kingdom!
All glory be to God!
Congratulations!
If you prayed that prayer, we would love to hear from you and bless you with some tools to equip you, and get you started on your new kingdom journey.

KINGDOMRIGHTS2.ORG

"Now the God of peace, that brought again from the dead our Lord Jesus, that great shepherd of the sheep, through the blood of the everlasting covenant, make you perfect in every good work to do his will, working in you that which is well pleasing in his sight, through Jesus Christ; to whom be glory for ever and ever...Amen."

www.ingramcontent.com/pod-product-compliance
Lightning Source LLC
Chambersburg PA
CBHW022008120726
47992CB00001B/479